Piece
in the
Hoop

20 quilt projects
+ 40 machine embroidery designs

Larisa Bland

KRAUSE PUBLICATIONS
CINCINNATI, OHIO

mycraftivity.com
connect. create. explore.

14 13 12 11 10   5 4 3 2 1

Distributed in Canada by Fraser Direct
100 Armstrong Avenue
Georgetown, ON, Canada L7G 5S4
Tel: (905) 877-4411

Distributed in the U.K. and Europe by David & Charles
Brunel House, Newton Abbot, Devon, TQ12 4PU, England
Tel: (+44) 1626 323200, Fax: (+44) 1626 323319
Email: postmaster@davidandcharles.co.uk

Distributed in Australia by Capricorn Link
P.O. Box 704, S. Windsor NSW, 2756 Australia
Tel: (02) 4577-3555

Bland, Larisa.
  Piece in the hoop : 20 quilt projects+40 machine embroidery designs / Larisa Bland.
     p. cm.
  Includes index.
  ISBN-13: 978-1-4402-0356-5 (pbk. : alk. paper)
  ISBN-10: 1-4402-0356-3 (pbk. : alk. paper)
  1. Patchwork--Patterns. 2. Embroidery--Design.. I. Title.
  TT835.B51345 2010
  746.46'041--dc22
                        2009037600

Edited by Vanessa Lyman
Production edited by Vanessa Lyman and Rachel Scheller
Designed by Julie Barnett and Steven Peters
Production coordinated by Greg Nock
Step-by-step photography by Christine Polomsky
Other photography, including cover, by Ric Deliantoni

www.fwmedia.com

ABOUT THE AUTHOR

I have been digitizing embroidery designs for almost nine years and quilting for as long as I can remember. As I grew up, I quilted less and less because it proved to be time consuming; it seemed I never could get a project finished. When I became pregnant with my daughter, I picked it up again and that's about the time I began digitizing.When I discovered that I could digitize a quilt block, I nearly fell off my chair. It was such a wild and fulfilling experience! I finally found a faster way to make a nearly perfect quilt. I added the block designs to my Web site (www.pieceinthehoop. com), which I developed from the ground up, and they took off. There's nothing like instant gratification projects to keep stitchers coming back for more! What once was a hobby for me has turned out to be a lucrative home-based business that just keeps growing.

Metric Conversion Chart

To convert	to	multiply by
Inches	Centimeters	2.54
Centimeters	Inches	0.4
Feet	Centimeters	30.5
Centimeters	Feet	0.03
Yards	Meters	0.9
Meters	Yards	1.1

Acknowledgments

I would like to thank the following people for their encouragement and support:

My Creator—Thank you, Lord, for giving me a talent that permits me to work from home with a flexible schedule so that I can be there for my family. Thank you for all my blessings. I give you full glory.

My Family—My mom, sisters Karen and Sandy, and Daniel for their help with the kids so that I could meet deadlines; my cousin Tammie Baggett for her love, extensive help, quilt stencil drawings and lots of quilting advice.

My Stitchers—My dear, true friend Sandy Kent, on whom I leaned for more than sewing. Thanks for stitching your heart out on several projects. Your opinions, hard work and dedication are greatly appreciated! To Angi Baker and Mary Jane Hetzlein for helping stitch blocks for projects. I couldn't have made it without you girls!

My Publishers and Staff—Vanessa Lyman for being patient and understanding, and for all her hard work organizing the book; Christine Polomsky for her wild personality and beautiful photography; Candy Wiza for pitching my idea and to everyone behind the scenes at Krause Publications and F+W Media that helped make my dream come to print.

My DVD Publisher—To Nancy Zieman for choosing me to work with her on this book; I'm honored. To Deanna Springer and Lois Kurtz for their hospitality, making Sandy Kent and I feel at home during our week-long visit to Wisconsin. I really enjoyed videographers Bruce Johnson and Steve Doebel, as well as Vicki Fischer, my makeup artist.

My Friends—DJ Caputo for always believing in me, Cindy Lee for her eye for color and knowledge of quilting, Lee Hall for his generosity, Veronica Cox for showing me the ropes and Rebecca Kemp Brent for assisting with the conversions.

I'd also like to thank the following companies for providing materials for the projects in this book: RNK Distributing, OLFA®, United Notions Moda, RJR Fabrics, Blank Quilting, Havel's Inc., June Tailor, Inc., Superior Threads, Clover Needlecraft, Inc., and Buzz Tools, Inc.

Dedication

I would like to dedicate this book to my children, Linsey Reece and Talon Dean.

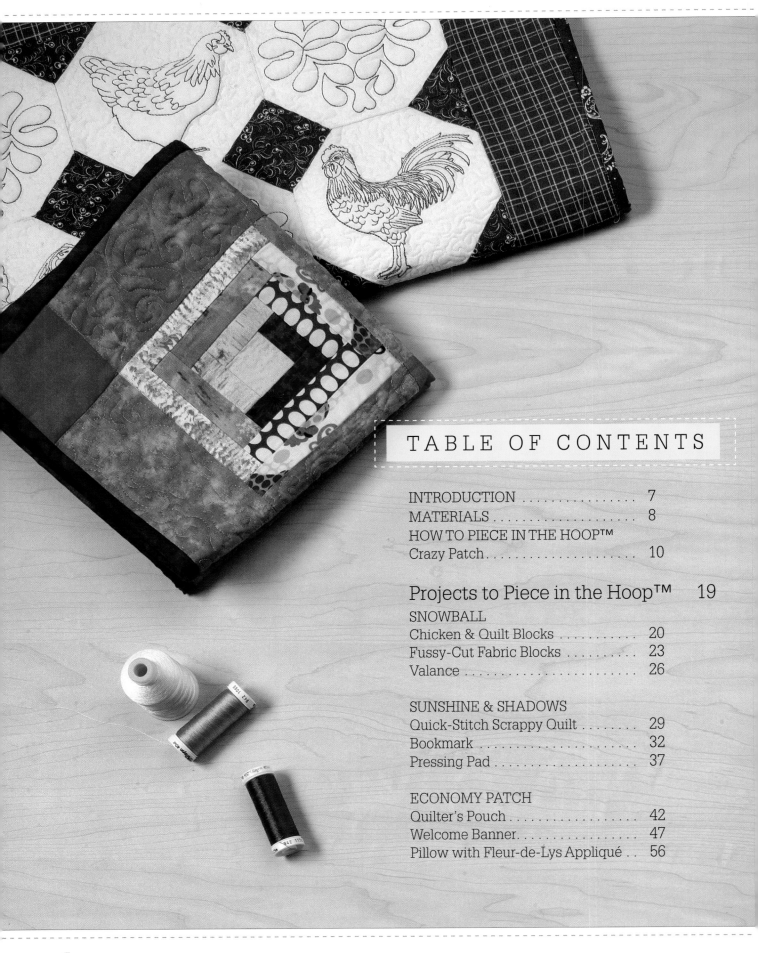

TABLE OF CONTENTS

Introduction

Piecing in the Hoop™ is a new, innovative way to make quilt blocks with an embroidery machine. This technique is precise, fast and lots of fun for all skill levels. All you have to do is add fabric and flip because the embroidery machine does all the sewing for you. Your resulting block will be nearly perfect every time! I will show you step by step how to Piece in the Hoop™, then we will turn your stitch-outs into interesting, attention-grabbing projects. Come, pull up a chair and let's get to Piecing in the Hoop™.

As part of the *Create with Nancy* line, this book contains extra helpful tips and a bonus DVD from sewing, quilting and embroidery expert Nancy Zieman. When you encounter a *Note from Nancy*, stop to read it—and be sure to watch the DVD to see the techniques in action!

NOTES FROM NANCY

Materials

In order to Piece in the Hoop™, you'll need to stock basic quilting and embroidery notions in your sewing studio. It is essential that you have the basic tools for quilting. You can spend a little or a lot on tools, but remember that you get what you pay for! New tools are created all the time to make our job easier, so visit your quilt store to view the latest and greatest gadgets.

Embroidery Machine
Your embroidery machine must have a hoop that is at least 5" × 7". Your machine must turn into a regular sewing machine for straight stitching. If it doesn't have this capability, you will need a regular sewing machine to complete some projects.

Temporary Adhesive Spray
(not pictured)
Temporary adhesive spray is a repositionable fabric adhesive used to temporarily bond fabrics.

Fusible Stabilizer
I recommend Floriani No Show Mesh Fusible stabilizer because it eliminates the need for a temporary spray adhesive. It holds all of the fabric pieces neatly and securely in place. The lightweight, no-show mesh stabilizer is not removed when the block is complete. Floriani also makes Stitch N Wash Fusible, a water-soluble stabilizer that dissolves once the project is washed. When using a fusible stabilizer while hooping, remember that the shiny side faces up.

Interfacing
Some projects need a heavier material to help them hold their shape. Cardstock or a heavy interfacing may work, but I find Timtex Stabilizer to be the most versatile. It is excellent for soft fabric crafts.

Irons
For the projects in this book, you'll need a mini craft iron for working in small places, and a home utility iron for pressing fabrics.

Quilter's Ruler
A transparent ruler with clearly marked ¼" markings is needed for squaring up blocks and fabric edges so you can cut them straight.

Rotary Cutter
A rotary cutter is used in conjunction with a straightedge ruler for cutting straight, accurate lines.

Scissors
You'll need fabric scissors for cutting larger pieces of fabric and curved embroidery scissors for cutting loose threads and appliqué seams.

Point Turner
For turning projects inside out, a point turner will give you crisp, accurate corners.

Tweezers
Tweezers are great for grasping loose threads that are too short to pick up.

Ribbon
I often use crafter's ribbon for hanging my quilt projects.

Pressing Pad
A pressing pad allows you to press your pieces back without removing the hoop from the machine. You simply place it between the stabilizer and the machine, and then use your mini iron to press. It is one of the handiest tools I have! Instructions for making one begin on page 37.

Piecework Pins
Use pins to keep fabric layers from shifting.

Tape

Use regular transparent tape to anchor ribbon and fabrics.

Thread

In this book, I most often use no. 50 weight cotton thread for piecing and assorted embroidery threads for redwork and appliqué work.

Lint Roller

This handy tool removes loose threads from your projects and work surfaces (and your clothes!) with ease.

Bobbins

Save time by winding several bobbins before you begin sewing.

Cutting Mat

A cutting mat serves as a base surface while cutting fabrics with a rotary cutter.

Needles

Always start out using a new needle. I use 80/12. Use whatever works best in your machine.

Fabric

(not pictured)

Good quality, 100 percent cotton fabrics are recommended for the projects in this book. As with all quilting projects, it is best to prewash your fabrics before getting started. This will take care of any fabric that shrinks a little. Some lesser-quality fabrics may allow underneath pieces to show through, ruining your block. For the *Pressing Pad* project, you will need ironing board cover fabric.

Batting

(not pictured)

Cotton batting has a low loft, producing a more antique look when it is quilted.

Fiberfill

(not pictured)

Use for stuffing pillows and craft projects.

Crazy Patch

This block showcases the Piece in the Hoop™ process. I've broken out the steps in detail to show you each stitched line, every trim, every piece flipped back and fused in place. Later projects won't be broken out in quite so much detail, but once you've walked through the crazy patch block, you should be ready to start piecing in the hoop!

FABRIC & THREAD
FABRIC FOR BLOCK
Eight scraps, measuring at least 2½" × 6" each

THREAD
Neutral cotton thread for piecing

EMBROIDERY DESIGN
crazypatch

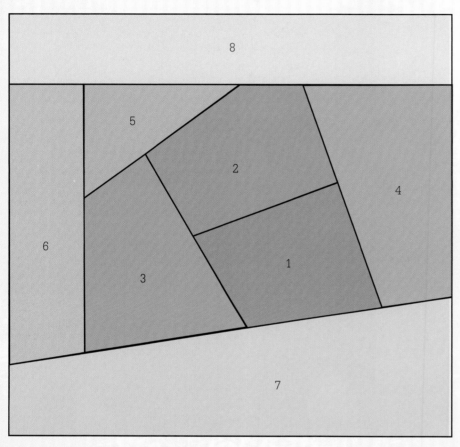

CRAZY PATCH FABRIC PLACEMENT CHART

NOTES FROM **NANCY**

If you have digitizing or embroidery software, print out the design files on the disk at 100% to enlarge or use for templates when cutting fabric pieces.

1 Lay out all your fabrics according to the placement chart on page 10.

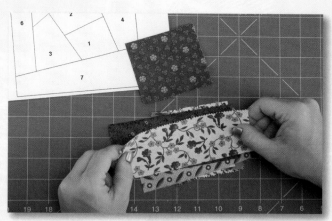

2 Set aside piece 1, then start a different stack with piece 2 face up, followed by piece 3, etc.

3 Flip the stack over (piece 2 will be on top, wrong side up), and place by your machine. Your fabrics will be in the order that you need them. You'll just need to grab and sew.

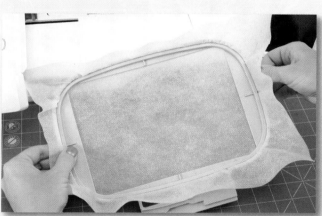

4 Hoop the stabilizer, ensuring that the fusible side is face up in the hoop. Place the hoop on the machine.

5 Load the design onto your machine and pull it up on the screen. Thread your machine. Use a neutral-colored thread for piecing; I've used black thread for visibility.

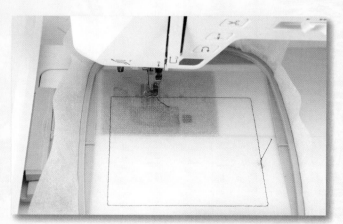

6 Allow the reference line to stitch. The reference line will indicate the overall shape of the final project. We will use it to square the block up once the block is finished.

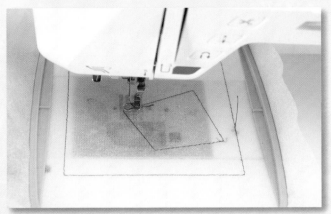

7 Start the machine and allow a placement shape to stitch. The placement shape indicates where you are to place fabric piece 1.

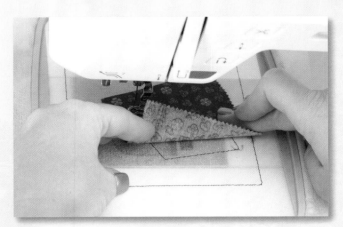

8 Position fabric piece 1 right side up over the placement shape. Ensure that the fabric extends past the placement shape on all sides, generally by about ¼".

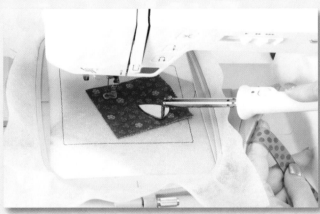

9 Slide a pressing pad (see page 37) under the hoop. Use a mini iron to fuse the fabric in place. Remove the pressing pad. If you prefer, you can remove the hoop from the machine, place it on an ironing board and use a mini iron or hobby iron to fuse the fabric in place. Return the hoop to the machine.

10 Start the machine and allow a placement line to stitch.

11 Grab piece 2 from the fabric stack and place it right side down over piece 1. Align the edge of piece 2 against the placement line. Ensure that piece 2 extends at least ¼" beyond both ends of the placement line.

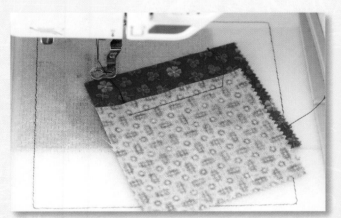

12 Start the machine and allow the tacking line to stitch. This will anchor piece 2 in place.

13 Using curved embroidery scissors, trim away the excess fabric of piece 1 right up to the placement line from Step 10.

14 Either slip a pressing pad under the hoop, or place it on an ironing board. Flip piece 2 back and fuse in place using a mini iron. Remove the pressing pad or return the hoop to the machine.

15 Start the machine and allow the next placement line to stitch.

16 Grab piece 3 from your stack and place it right side down along the placement line. Ensure that piece 3 extends at least ¼" beyond both ends of the placement line. Start the machine and allow the tacking line to stitch, anchoring piece 3 in place.

17 Trim away the excess fabric along the placement line from Step 15, removing the hoop from the machine if necessary.

18 Either slip a pressing pad under the hoop, or remove it from the machine and place it on an ironing board. Flip back fabric piece 3 and fuse in place using a mini iron. Remove the pressing pad or return the hoop to the machine.

19 Start the machine and allow a placement line to stitch.

20 Grab piece 4 from the fabric stack and place it right side down along the placement line. Ensure that piece 4 extends at least ¼" beyond both ends of the placement line. Start the machine and allow a tacking line to stitch, anchoring piece 4.

21 Trim away the excess fabric along the placement line from Step 19, removing the hoop from the machine if necessary.

22 Either slip a pressing pad under the hoop, or remove the hoop from the machine and place it on an ironing board. Flip back fabric piece 4 and fuse in place using a mini iron. Remove the pressing pad or return the hoop to the machine.

23 Start the machine and allow the next placement line to stitch.

24 Grab piece 5 from the fabric stack and place it right side down along the placement line. Ensure that piece 5 extends at least ¼" beyond both ends of the placement line. Start the machine and allow the tacking line to stitch, anchoring piece 5 in place.

25 Trim away the excess fabric along the placement line from Step 23, removing the hoop from the machine if necessary.

26 Either slip a pressing pad under the hoop, or remove the hoop from the machine and place it on an rioning board. Flip back fabric piece 5 and fuse in place using a mini iron. Remove the pressing pad or return the hoop to the machine.

27 Start the machine and allow the next placement line to stitch.

28 Grab piece 6 from the fabric stack and place it right side down along the placement line. Ensure that piece 6 extends at least ¼" beyond both ends of the placement line. Start the machine and allow the tacking line to stitch, anchoring piece 6 in place.

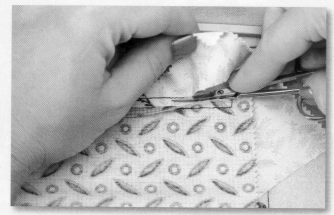

29 Trim away the excess fabric along the placement line from Step 27, removing the hoop from the machine if necessary.

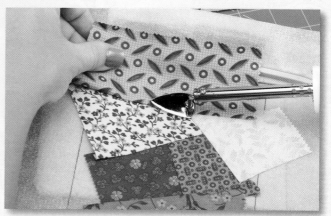

30 Either slip a pressing pad under the hoop, or remove the hoop from the machine and place it on an ironing board. Flip back fabric piece 6 and fuse in place using a mini iron. Remove the pressing pad or return the hoop to the machine.

31 Start the machine and allow the next placement line to stitch.

32 Grab piece 7 from the fabric stack and place it right side down along the placement line. Ensure that piece 7 extends at least ¼" beyond both ends of the placement line. Start the machine and allow the tacking line to stitch, anchoring piece 7 in place.

33 Trim away the excess fabric along the placement line from Step 31, removing the hoop from the machine if necessary.

34 Either slip a pressing pad under the hoop, or remove the hoop from the machine and place it on an ironing board. Flip back fabric piece 7 and fuse in place using a mini iron. Remove the pressing pad or return the hoop to the machine.

35 Start the machine and allow the next placement line to stitch.

36 Grab piece 8 from the fabric stack and place it right side down along the placement line. Ensure that piece 8 extends at least ¼" beyond both ends of the placement line. Start the machine and allow the tacking line to stitch, anchoring piece 8 in place.

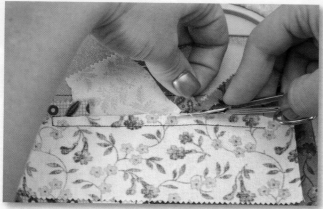

37 Trim away the excess fabric along the placement line from Step 35, removing the hoop from the machine if necessary.

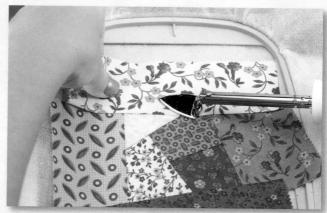

38 Either slip a pressing pad under the hoop, or remove the hoop from the machine and place on an ironing board. Flip back fabric piece 8 and fuse it in place using a mini iron. Remove the pressing pad or return the hoop to the machine.

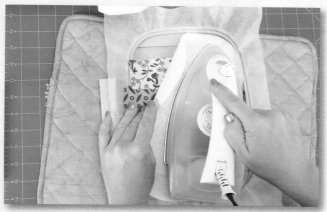

39 Remove the hoop from the machine and place it on a pressing pad. Cover the block with a press cloth or appliqué pressing sheet to avoid getting adhesive from the fusible web on the iron. Don't use steam!

40 Remove the block from the hoop and flip it over. Measure ¼" past the reference line.

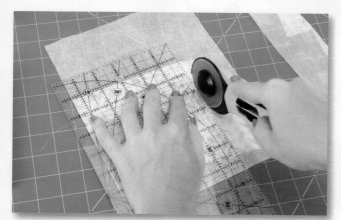

41 Cut off the excess from all four sides.

42 Your final block should be pretty much perfect!

Projects to Piece in the Hoop™

The instructions to follow are organized from the simplest block design to the one with the most fabric pieces. Don't let the number of pieces intimidate you, because this technique is truly easy and effortless. Each block design comes with three different projects that show various ways it can be used. The last section features projects made by combining different block designs.

This book provides you with a foundation and a number of building blocks to spark your creativity so you can develop your own projects. I've included a few special block designs that may be appliquéd on almost any item. Try combining blocks to make full-size quilts, wall hangings or even table runners. The beauty of my piecing technique is that it doesn't limit you to just making quilts; rather, it allows you to create all kinds of fun, exciting, quick-sew items.

Chicken & Quilt Blocks

This fun wall hanging combines the Snowball block design with bluework embroidery and quilting motifs. On the disk, I've included the bluework design without the snowball block (bonusqdes1) for those of you who would like to use this design for quilting additional projects.

21" × 21"

FABRIC & THREAD

FABRIC FOR BLOCKS

Nine 5½" squares for the background

Eighteen 2⅜" squares, cut diagonally to produce thirty-six triangles

FABRIC FOR BORDERS

Two 3½" × 16" strips

Two 3½" × 24" strips

FABRIC FOR BACKING

One 26" square

FABRIC FOR BINDING

One strip, approximately 5½" × 40"

BATTING

One 26" square

THREAD

Neutral thread for piecing

Embroidery thread for bluework (if you like a more hand-stitched look, use a cotton thread)

EMBROIDERY DESIGNS

snowchik1

snowchik2

snowchik3

snowchik4

snowchikmtf

bonusqdes1*

*Watch the DVD to see how this bonus quilting/embroidery design is used in an additional project!

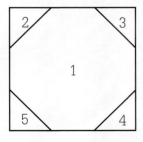

SNOWBALL FABRIC
PLACEMENT CHART

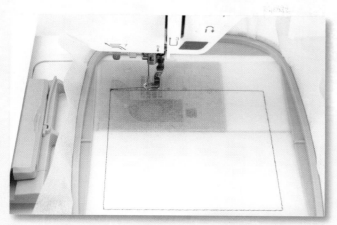

1 Load designs snowchik1 through snowchik4, and snowchikmtf onto your machine. Thread the machine using a neutral thread. (I've used black thread here for visibility.) Hoop the stabilizer. Pull up the piecing design (snowchk3). Start the machine to allow the reference line square to stitch.

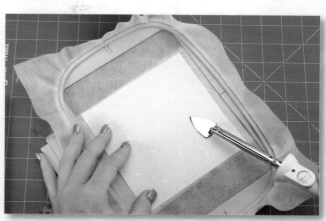

2 Remove the hoop from the machine. Place the background fabric, right side up, over the reference line square, making sure the square is completely covered. No stitches should be visible. Slip a pressing pad under the hoop, and then use a mini iron to fuse the background fabric in place.

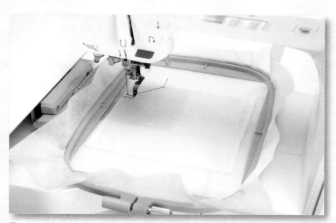

3 Return the hoop to the machine. Now begins the stitch-n-flip section of this design. Please refer to the fabric placement chart on page 20 for the stitching order. Start your machine and allow a placement line to stitch.

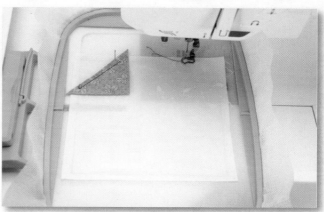

4 Place a triangle right side down along the placement line. Ensure that the triangle extends at least ¼" beyond both ends of the placement line. Start the machine and allow a tacking line to stitch.

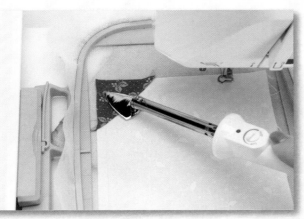

5 Slip a pressing pad under the hoop. Using the mini iron, press the triangle back, fusing it in place. Remove the pressing pad. Trim away the excess fabric as needed.

6 Refer to the placement chart to place the next piece. Repeat this process until all four corners have been placed.

7 Once the block is complete, change to your embroidery thread. Allow the chicken bluework design to stitch out. Repeat with remaining designs. We will create nine Snowball blocks total: four with chickens in bluework and five with the quilting design in bluework.

8 Remove each block from the hoop and flip it upside down so you are looking at the stabilizer side. Locate the reference line square. Using a quilter's ruler and a rotary cutter, trim ¼" outside the reference line square on all sides.

Putting the Project Together

When you're ready to put the quilt top together, switch to your sewing machine.

To create the quilt top, arrange blocks to create the following pattern:

Row 1: Quilt Motif + Chicken + Quilt Motif

Row 2: Chicken + Quilt Motif + Chicken

Row 3: Quilt Motif + Chicken + Quilt Motif

There is no sashing between the blocks. Sew Row 1 together, then Row 2, then Row 3.

Next, sew Row 1 to Row 2 and press the seams open. Sew Row 3 to Row 2 and press the seams open.

For borders, stitch one 3½" × 16" strip to the top, and one strip to the bottom. Press the seams back and trim excess. Stitch one 3½" × 24" strip to the left, and one strip to the right of the combined blocks. Press the seams back and trim the excess. Layer backing, batting and quilt top. Pin and quilt the layers together, then add the binding.

Fussy-Cut Fabric Blocks

There are so many fabrics out there with fun prints that you would just love to frame. I chose the Snowball block just for that. You can center cute prints in the middle of the block, then stitch the corners directly onto it. Since this block sews out super fast, it's nothing to stitch twelve blocks together to make a little quilt.

25" × 31"

FABRIC & THREAD

FABRIC FOR BLOCKS

Twelve 6" squares of fussy-cut novelty print

Forty-eight 2" × 2¾" rectangles

FABRIC FOR BORDERS

Two 3½" × 21" strips

Two 3½" × 34" strips

FABRIC FOR SASHING

Eight 1½" × 5½" strips

Two 1½" × 27" strips

Two 1½" × 19" strips

FABRIC FOR BACKING

One 26" square

FABRIC FOR BINDING

One strip, approximately 6" × 40"

BATTING

One 27" × 33" rectangle

THREAD

Neutral cotton thread for piecing

EMBROIDERY DESIGN

snowfusscut

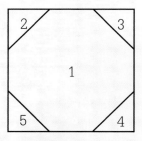

SNOWBALL FABRIC
PLACEMENT CHART

1 Start by fussy-cutting your fabric for the Snowball blocks. Isolate the print motif in the fabric that you want to feature in your fussy-cut block. Here, I picked this happy, green-shirted cowboy. Using your quilter's ruler, center the motif in a 5" square.

2 Use a quilter's ruler and a rotary cutter to cut twelve 6" fabric squares, making sure your desired print is centered. I allowed a little extra.

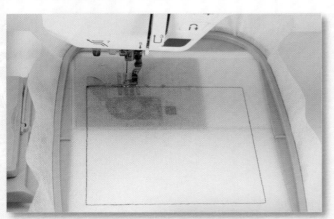

3 Load the design onto your machine. Thread the machine using a neutral thread. (I've used black thread here for visibility.) Hoop the stabilizer. Pull up the piecing design (snowfusscut). Start the machine and allow the reference line square to stitch.

4 Remove the hoop from the machine. Place the fussy-cut fabric, centered right side up, over the reference line square, making sure the square is completely covered. No stitches should be visible. Slip a pressing pad under the hoop, and then use a mini iron to fuse the fabric in place.

5 Refer to the fabric placement chart on page 23 for the stitching order. Now comes the stitch-n-flip section of this design. Place the hoop back on the machine. Start the machine and allow a placement line to stitch.

6 Place a rectangle right side down along the placement line. Ensure that the rectangle extends at least ¼" beyond both ends of the placement line. Start the machine and allow a tacking line to stitch. After the tacking line has stitched, slip a pressing pad under the hoop, flip the fabric back and use the mini iron to fuse the fabric in place. Remove the pressing pad.

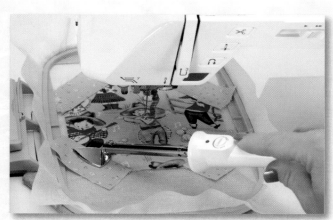

7 Repeat this process until all four pieces of fabric are secured.

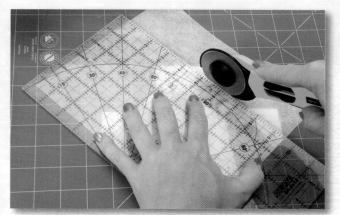

8 Remove the block from the hoop and turn it upside down. Viewing the stabilizer side of the block, locate the reference line square. Use a quilter's ruler and rotary cutter to trim ¼" outside the reference square. Create a total of twelve Snowball blocks.

Putting the Project Together

When you're ready to put the quilt top together, switch to your sewing machine. To create the quilt top, arrange the blocks in four rows and three columns (see finished project on page 23). Each row should be arranged like this:

block + 1½" × 5½" sashing + block + 1½" × 5½" sashing + block

Do this for all four rows. Neatly press.

Take the five 1½" × 19" strips and add them between the rows, and then to the top and bottom. Press the seams back and trim the excess.

To complete the sashing, attach the 1½" × 27" strips to the left and right. Neatly press the entire top.

To finish the top, simply stitch the two 3½" × 21" strips to top and bottom. Press seams back and trim the excess. Stitch the two 3½" × 34" strips to each side. Press seams back and trim excess. Finish as desired.

Valance

Add the final touch to your window treatment with a custom valance. You can use the design shown here, or you can personalize your project by importing a favorite embroidery design to fit a 5" × 5" area. You can also use the provided embroidery motif to quilt on any item. Simply place a water-soluble stabilizer such as Vilene in the hoop, then place the sandwiched quilt on the hoop and pin it to the stabilizer. Use blendable threads for both the bobbin and the top quilting threads. Allow the motif to stitch in your desired location.

TIP: For a hand-stitched look, run two strands of cotton thread through your machine at one time.

12" × 31"

FABRIC & THREAD

FABRIC FOR BLOCKS

Five 6" light gold squares

Ten 3" medium gold squares, cut diagonally to produce twenty triangles

FABRIC FOR SASHING AND BORDERS

Six 1½" × 5" black sashing strips

One 4½" × 32" black border strip

One 6½" × 32" black border strip

FABRIC FOR BACKING

One 12" × 34" black strip, folded on one edge 1" to produce 12" x 33"

One 4" × 12" black strip

THREAD

Black embroidery thread for the entire project

EMBROIDERY DESIGN

snowvalance

bonusqdes2

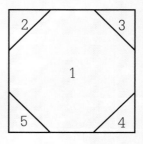

SNOWBALL FABRIC
PLACEMENT CHART

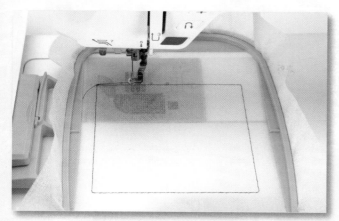

1 Load the designs onto your machine. Thread the machine using a neutral thread. (I've used black thread here for visibility.) Hoop the stabilizer. Pull up the piecing design (snowvalance). Start the machine and allow the reference line square to stitch.

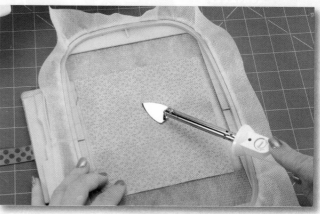

2 Remove the hoop from the machine. Place the background fabric, right side up, over the reference line square, making sure the square is completely covered. No stitches should be visible. Slip a pressing pad under the hoop, and then use a mini iron to fuse the background fabric in place.

3 Return the hoop to the machine. Now begins the stitch-n-flip section of this design. Refer to the fabric placement chart on page 26 for the stitching order. Start your machine and allow a placement line to stitch.

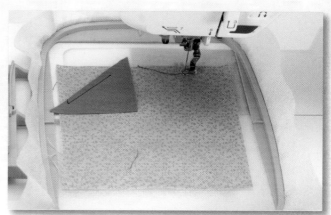

4 Place a triangle right side down along the placement line. Ensure that the triangle extends at least ¼" beyond both ends of the placement line. Start the machine and allow a tacking line to stitch.

5 When all four corners are tacked in place, remove the hoop from the machine and trim the excess using curved scissors.

6 Slip a pressing pad under the hoop. Use the mini iron to neatly press back the corners, fusing them in place.

7 Now you are ready to stitch the motif. If you wish to use your own design, pull it up now. Stitch out.

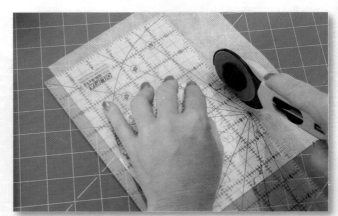

8 Remove the block from the hoop and turn it upside down. Viewing the stabilizer side of the block, locate the reference line square. Use a quilter's ruler and rotary cutter to trim ¼" outside the reference square. Repeat the steps to create a total of five Snowball blocks.

Putting the Project Together

When you're ready to put the valance together, switch to your sewing machine. Sew the 1½" × 5½" sashing strips to the blocks as shown in the finished project (see page 26).

Next, sew the 4½" × 32" border strip to the bottom. Take the 6½" × 32" border strip and fold in 1" on each end, then fold it in half and press to mark the center. Pin the raw edge to the top, right sides together, matching the fold to the center of the valance and allowing approximately ½" from the edge of the valance on each side. Stitch in place.

To create the pillow sham-style backing, take the 12" × 33" folded piece of fabric and place right side down, making sure it completely covers one end of the valance. Then place the 4" × 12", right side down, overlapping the folded edge and outer edge of the valance.

Stitch around all edges and turn inside out. Neatly press.

To create a rod pocket, run a stitch 1" from the top fold.

Quick-Stitch Scrappy Quilt

Here's a fun wall hanging that you can create with fabrics pulled from your scrap bin at random. It's a wonderful way to use up scraps and will brighten any room. Nancy and I used this quilt as a table throw on the DVD. It's just the perfect size to use in any area of your home or office.

26" × 26"

FABRIC & THREAD

FABRIC FOR BLOCKS
Ninety-six strips of scrappy fabric, up to 1" × 7½"

Sixteen 6" × 7¾" triangles

FABRIC FOR BORDERS
Two 3½" × 21" strips

Two 3½" × 27" strips

FABRIC FOR BACKING
One 30" square

FABRIC FOR BINDING
One strip, approximately 5½" × 40"

BATTING
One 30" square

THREAD
Neutral cotton thread for piecing

EMBROIDERY DESIGN
sunscrappy

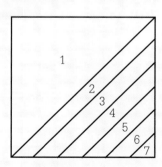

SUNSHINE & SHADOWS
QUILT FABRIC
PLACEMENT CHART

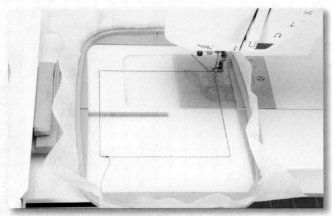

1 Load the design (sunscrappy) and thread the machine. Hoop the stabilizer. Start the machine and allow the reference line square to stitch.

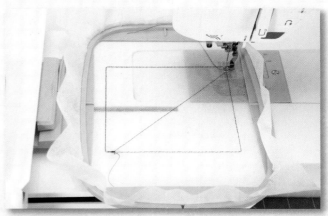

2 Start the machine and allow a triangle to stitch. This shows you where to place piece 1.

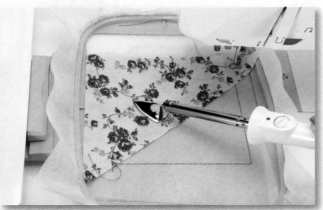

3 Place a fabric triangle, right side up, over the triangle created by the placement line. Make sure the fabric covers the entire triangle, so that no stitched edges are visible. Slip a pressing pad under the hoop and use your mini iron to fuse the fabric in place. Remove the pressing pad.

4 Now begins the stitch-n-flip section of this design. Refer to the fabric placement chart on page 29 for the stitching order. Start your machine and allow a placement line to stitch.

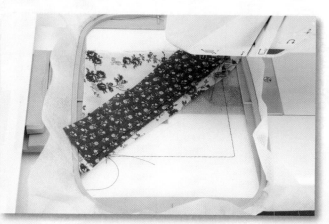

5 Place one of the 1" fabric scraps right side down along the placement line. Ensure the fabric scrap extends at least ¼" beyond both ends of the placement line. Start your machine and allow the tacking line to stitch. Trim any excess.

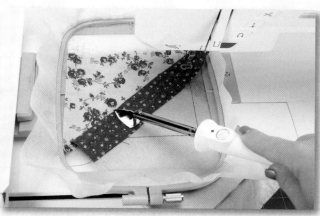

6 Slip a pressing pad under the hoop, flip the fabric back, and use the mini iron to fuse the fabrics together. Remove the pressing pad.

7 Start the machine and allow a placement line to stitch. Follow the placement chart for the sequence. Repeat this process until all seven pieces of fabric have been secured.

8 Remove the block from the hoop and turn it upside down. Viewing the stabilizer side of the block, locate the reference line square that first stitched. Using a quilter's ruler and rotary cutter, trim ¼" outside of all sides. Make a total of sixteen blocks.

Putting the Project Together

Take four of the 5" scrappy blocks and arrange them in a square, so that the small points create a diamond effect. Stitch together to create a 10" block. Repeat to create three other blocks. Stitch two of the 10" blocks together. Repeat for the other two blocks, then stitch these rows together. To add the borders, sew one 3" × 21" strip of border material along the top, and one along the bottom using a ¼" seam allowance. Press back and trim off the ends. Stitch the two remaining border strips to the left and right sides using a ¼" seam allowance. Press back and trim off the ends. Finish as desired.

Bookmark

This is a very quick project to stitch, and can be done all in one hooping. After the stitch-n-flip process is complete, you'll add two pieces of fabric to the back. When this is done, turn the project inside out, and you will have a completed bookmark with a pouch for holding pencils or even reading glasses.

2½" × 7"

FABRIC & THREAD

FABRIC FOR BLOCKS
Three 2½" × 4" rectangles

Twenty-one strips, ¾" wide and up to 4" long

FABRIC FOR BACKING
One 3" × 7½" rectangle

One 2" × 3" rectangle

THREAD
Neutral cotton thread for piecing

EMBROIDERY DESIGN
sunbkmrk

SUNSHINE & SHADOWS
BOOKMARK FABRIC
PLACEMENT CHART

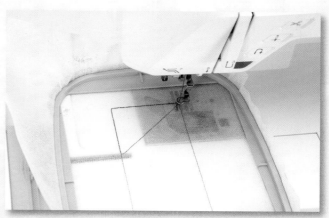

1 Load the designs onto your machine. Thread the machine using a neutral thread. (I've used black thread here for visibility.) Hoop the stabilizer. Pull up the piecing design (sunbkmrk). Start the machine to allow the reference line square to stitch.

2 Start the machine and allow the placement triangle to stitch.

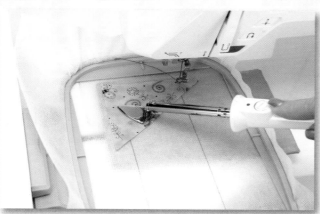

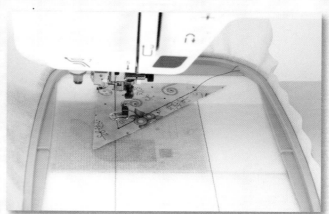

3 Slip a pressing pad under the hoop. Place a 2½" × 4" fabric triangle over the stitched triangle, right side up, making sure no stitching is visible. Using the mini iron, fuse the piece in place.

4 Now begins the stitch-n-flip section of this design. Refer to the fabric placement chart on page 32 for the stitching order. Start the machine and allow a placement line to stitch.

5 Place a ¾" fabric strip right side down along the placement line. Ensure that the fabric strip extends at least ¼" beyond both ends of the placement line. Start your machine and allow a tacking line to stitch.

6 Trim as closely to the tacking line as possible. It's important to trim as you go, especially in small projects like this with lots of fabrics. The seams could easily become messy with so many fabrics bulking them up. Slip a pressing pad under the hoop. Flip the fabric back and use the mini iron to fuse the fabric in place. Remove the pressing pad.

NOTES FROM NANCY

Piecing in the hoop can cover a multitude of sins, but the fabric pieces must be larger than the placement outline. If the fabric doesn't quite extend past the stitched outline, the shorter piece must be removed. So, carefully clip the stitches and replace the fabric with a larger piece. It's a simple fix!

7 Repeat this process until all seven pieces are in place. Follow the fabric placement chart for the stitching order.

8 When the first section of the bookmark is complete, start the machine and allow the next horizontal placement line to stitch.

9 Place a 2½" × 4" triangle piece right side down along the placement line. Start the machine and allow a tacking line to stitch. Trim away the excess. Slip a pressing pad under the hoop. Using your mini iron, fuse the fabric in place.

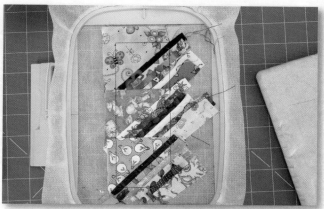

10 Repeat the stitch-n-flip sequence until all of the fabric pieces have been placed. Start the machine and allow the reference line rectangle to stitch again. This defines the boundaries for the back material. Remove the hoop from the machine.

NOTES FROM **NANCY**

Trimming is an important step that works best when you can get close to your work and trim next to the tacking line. It is often easier to release and remove the hoop from the machine before trimming.

11 Place the 3" × 7½" strip on a pressing pad. With wrong sides together, fold the top down 1" and press. This will create a 3" × 6½" rectangle. Place this fabric approximately ½" below the top of the stitched rectangle, right side down with the fold pointed upward. Place the 2" × 3" strip right side down over the top. Make sure this strip overlaps the fold by at least 1". The folded fabric pieces should cover the reference shape completely.

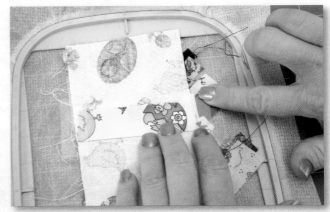

12 Use tape to secure the fabric, especially at the fold overlap. Return the hoop to the machine.

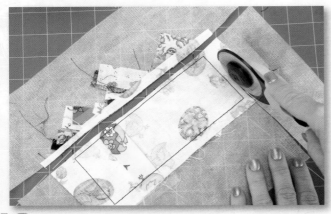

13 Start the machine and allow a double outside rectangle shape to stitch. Remove the project from the hoop. Trim ¼" to ⅛" from the outside of the stitched rectangle. Use a ruler as a guide if you prefer.

14 Nip the corners. This will help ensure crisper, less bulky corners. Turn the project inside out. Use a point turner to help turn out the corners. Press the project with a regular or hobby iron.

Pressing Pad

This little pad has multiple uses. It works as a hot pad for your kitchen or as a pressing pad for your sewing area. Teflon fabric is a silvery-colored material used for objects such as ironing board covers that need to withstand high temperatures.

4¾" × 6¾"

FABRIC & THREAD

FABRIC FOR BLOCKS

Six strips of 1930s reproduction fabrics, 1½" wide and up to 9" long

One 5½" × 7½" rectangle of unbleached muslin

FABRIC FOR BACKING

One 5½" × 8" piece of Teflon fabric

One 2" × 5½" piece of Teflon fabric

BATTING

One 5½" × 7½" rectangle

OTHER

One 3½" piece of 1" wide ribbon

THREAD

Coordinating embroidery thread for the design

Neutral cotton thread for piecing

EMBROIDERY DESIGN
sunpresspad

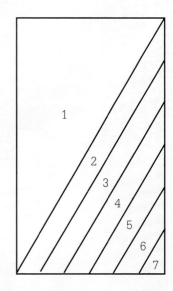

SUNSHINE & SHADOWS
PRESSING PAD FABRIC
PLACEMENT CHART

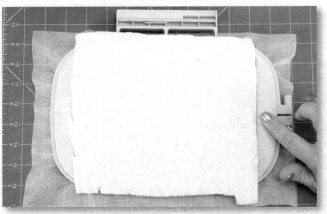

1 Load the design (sunpresspad) and thread the machine. (I've used black thread for visibility.) Hoop the stabilizer. Flip the hoop over and place the batting on the bottom of the stabilizer. Secure the batting with a temporary spray adhesive.

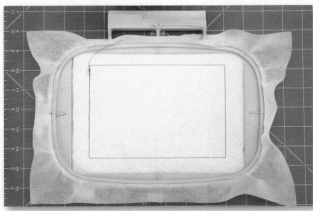

2 Put the hoop on the machine. Start the machine and allow a tacking line rectangle to stitch. Remove the hoop from the machine and trim the batting next to the stitched rectangle. Place the hoop back on the machine.

3 Using curved scissors, trim the batting as close to the tacking line as possible. Return the hoop to the machine.

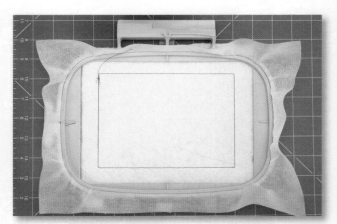

4 Start the machine and allow the larger reference line rectangle to stitch out. This will serve as the cutting line at the end of the project.

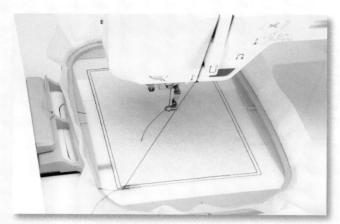

5 Start the machine and allow a triangle to stitch.

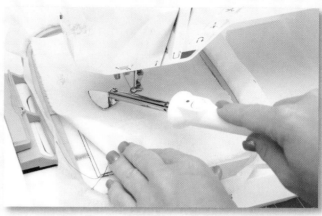

6 Lay the unbleached muslin square over the rectangle. Slip a pressing pad under the hoop, or remove the hoop from the machine and lay it on an ironing board. Fuse the fabric in place using the mini iron.

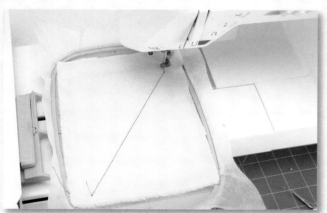

7 Now begins the stitch-n-flip section of this design. Refer to the fabric placement chart on page 37 for the stitching order. Return the hoop to the machine if needed. Start the machine and allow a placement line to stitch.

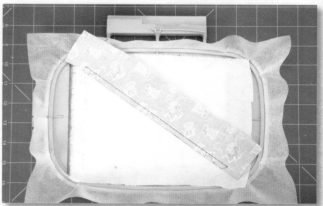

8 Place a 1½" fabric strip right side down along the placement line. Ensure that the fabric strip extends at least ¼" beyond both ends of the placement line. Start the machine and allow a tacking line to stitch. Remove the hoop from the machine.

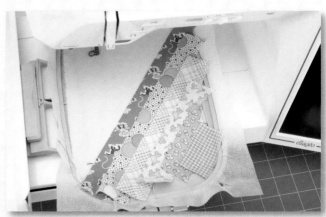

9 Trim away the excess muslin using your curved scissors. Trim as close to the tacking line as possible. When the excess is trimmed away, flip back the scrap fabric and fuse in place using a mini iron.

10 Place the hoop back on the machine. Continue the stitch-n-flip process until all seven reproduction fabrics have been placed. Follow the placement chart for the fabric sequence.

11 Load coordinating embroidery thread. Start the machine and allow the design to stitch out. Use your curved scissors to cut jump threads as needed.

12 After the design has finished stitching, load the cotton thread again, or continue using embroidery thread if you prefer. Start the machine and allow the reference line rectangle to stitch again.

13 To add the ribbon, remove the hoop from the machine. Position the folded ribbon in the center along the top edge, with the loop pointing down and the raw edge overlapping the rectangle by ½". Tape the ribbon in place to keep it from shifting.

14 Take the 5½" × 8" Teflon piece and fold the edge down about 1", wrong sides together. Press to crease. Position this piece, right side down, with the folded edge approximately 1" below the top of the stitched rectangle. Make sure that the rest of the reference line rectangle is covered. Place the 2" × 5½" Teflon piece right side down over the first, making sure the fold is overlapped by a minimum of 1" and the remaining fabric covers the rest of the rectangle. Use tape to secure all the pieces, especially the fold overlap.

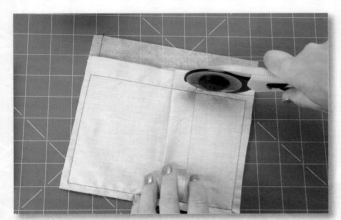

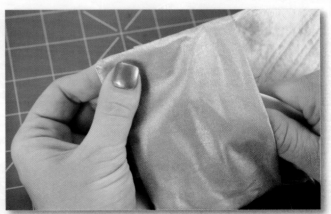

15 Replace the hoop on the machine. Start the machine and allow a double-run rectangle to stitch. Remove the project from the hoop. Using a rotary cutter, trim ¼" from the outside of the stitched rectangle. Use a ruler if you prefer.

16 Using a rotary cutter, nip the corners. This eliminates bulk, making it easier to achieve sharp corners. Turn the project inside out. Use the point turner to help turn the corners. Press neatly.

Quilter's Pouch

This design is very versatile. I added a long piece of ribbon so it can be worn around the neck to quilt shows to store your driver's license, credit cards or business cards. You can program your embroidery machine to stitch out your name and quilt guild, or import a favorite embroidery design. If you shorten the ribbon, this design will make a cute sachet to hang anywhere.

5" × 5"

FABRIC & THREAD

FABRIC FOR BLOCKS

One 3" square for the center

Two 3½" squares, cut diagonally to create four inside triangles

Two 4" squares, cut diagonally to create the four outside triangles

FABRIC FOR BACKING

One 5½" × 6½" rectangle

One 2½" × 5½" rectangle

OTHER

One 38" piece of ribbon

One 4¾" square of Timtex, cardboard or other stiff material

THREAD

Embroidery thread for the design

Neutral cotton thread for piecing

EMBROIDERY DESIGN
econpouch

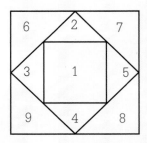

ECONOMY PATCH FABRIC
PLACEMENT CHART

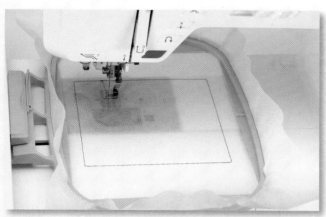

1 Load the design onto the machine. Thread the machine. (I've used black thread here for visibility.) Hoop the stabilizer, then start the machine and allow the reference square to stitch.

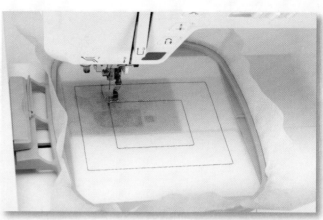

2 Start the machine and allow the placement shape to stitch.

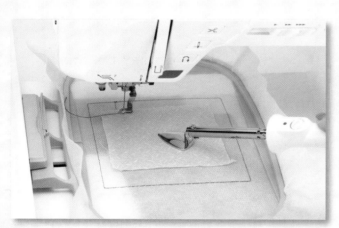

3 Place the 3" center fabric square right side up over the placement shape. Make sure the entire small square is covered. Slide your pressing pad under the hoop. Press the fabric in place using a mini iron. Remove the pressing pad.

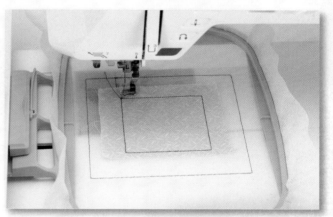

4 Start the machine and allow the tacking line to stitch. These stitches anchor the center square and prevent the fabric from puckering when you add the embroidery.

Generally you don't think of using embroidery thread when creating a patchwork project. Yet, this convenient Quilter's Pouch is a non-heirloom project. Save time and use embroidery thread as the needle thread for the entire project!

NOTES FROM **NANCY**

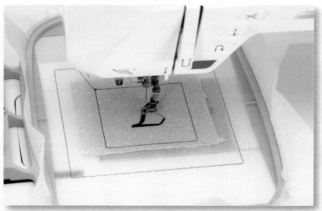

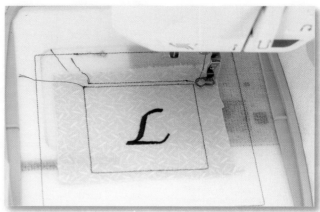

5 Add the embroidered text or design now. If a problem were to occur with the embroidery, you could start over without losing most of your piecing work. I chose to stitch out a simple *L* pulled from the machine's library of fonts, but you could insert your name and quilt guild. If you prefer, skip the embroidery and use a fabric pen to write directly on the fabric square.

6 Now begins the stitch-n-flip section of this design. Please refer to the fabric placement chart on page 42 for the stitching order. Change to cotton thread. Start your machine and allow a placement line to stitch.

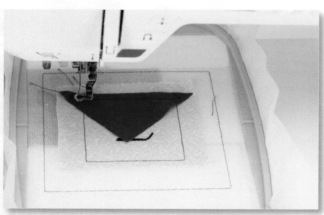

7 Place an inside triangle right side down along the placement line. Ensure that the triangle extends at least ¼" beyond both ends of the placement line. Start the machine and allow a tacking line to stitch. Notice that you don't always have to trim and remove the excess fabric. I do recommend doing so when creating quilts.

8 Slip the pressing pad under the hoop. Press the fabric back with your mini iron, fusing it in place. Trim away the excess fabric as needed.

NOTES FROM NANCY

If you'd like to learn how to add a monogram to the Piece in the Hoop™ design, click on Economy Patch on the Main Menu screen of the DVD. Larisa will walk you through the process!

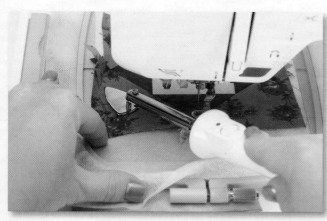

9 Follow the fabric placement chart for the sequence. Repeat the process until all nine pieces have been placed.

10 When all nine pieces have been placed and fused, start your machine and allow the large reference line square to stitch out again. You can use the point turner or some tape to keep the fabric from getting caught in the foot.

11 Tape one end of the ribbon right side down in the top-left corner, about ½" from the left side of the reference line. Do the same on the right side. Allow the raw edges of the ribbon to extend about 1" beyond the stitching line. Make sure the ribbon loop is completely inside the large stitched square; bunch it up and tape it securely in place.

12 Position the 5½" × 6½" backing fabric right side down on the pressing pad. Fold the top down 1½" and press. You should now have a 5" × 5½" fabric square. Place this right side down on top of the square, about 1" from the top of the large stitched square. The other sides of the fabric should overlap the square by at least ¼".

NOTES FROM NANCY

If you're using a satin or printed ribbon, place the shiny or print side down. After the stitching is complete, the pretty part of the ribbon will be visible.

13 Place the remaining 2½" × 5½" piece of backing fabric right side down, overlapping the fold by at least 1¼". This fabric should overlap the top and sides of the square by at least ¼". Using tape, secure the two pieces of fabric to keep them from shifting. Place tape where they overlap, too.

14 Start the machine and the reference square will double run, tacking the overlapped fabrics to the finished block. Remove the tape and the project from the hoop. Trim to ¼" around all sides. Clip the corners.

15 Turn inside out, using a point turner for crisp corners. Neatly press. Insert Timtex or cardboard to keep the pouch stiff. Make sure to wear this to your next quilt show!

Welcome Banner

I've combined several of the techniques that we've learned thus far to create a hanging banner. We're piecing, adding text and ribbon, then creating a pillow sham effect. You can replace WELCOME with your own letters to spell out anything. This banner can be hung so that upon arriving your guest will be welcomed by your creativity.

11" × 44½"

FABRIC & THREAD

FABRIC FOR BLOCKS

Seven 3" squares for the centers

Fourteen 3" squares cut diagonally to produce the twenty-eight inner triangles

Fourteen 4" squares, cut diagonally to produce twenty-eight outer triangles

FABRIC FOR TOP & SIDE BORDERS

One 3½" × 13" strip

Two 3½" × 36" strips

FABRIC FOR BOTTOM BORDER

One 12½" square

FABRIC FOR BACKING

One 14" × 49" rectangle

One 5" × 14" rectangle

BATTING

One 14" × 47" rectangle

OTHER

One 10" piece of 1–1½" wide ribbon

6" × 10⅞" piece of fusible interfacing

THREAD

Embroidery thread for the design

Neutral cotton thread for piecing

EMBROIDERY DESIGN

econbannerc

econbannere

econbannerl

econbannerm

econbannero

econbannerw

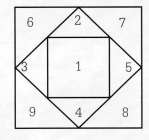

ECONOMY PATCH FABRIC
PLACEMENT CHART

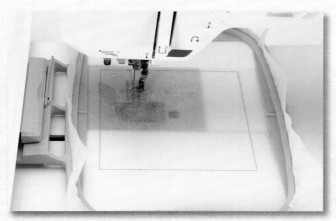

1 Load the design and thread the machine. You can use the same thread throughout, if you like. Hoop the stabilizer. Start the machine and allow the reference square to stitch.

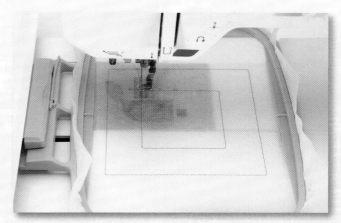

2 Start the machine and allow the placement square to stitch.

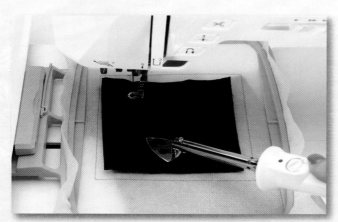

3 Place the 3" center fabric square right side up on the small placement square. Make sure the entire small square is covered. Slip a pressing pad under the hoop, then fuse the fabric in place using a mini iron. Remove the pressing pad.

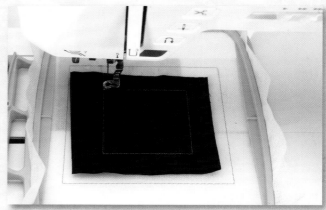

4 Start the machine and the same tacking lines will stitch, anchoring the center square.

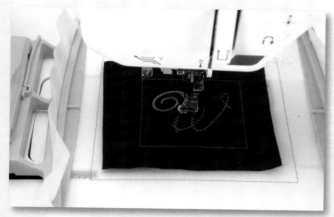

5 At this stage of each block, embroider the design. If something goes wrong with the embroidery at this stage, it'll be easy enough to start over. Start the machine and allow the letter to stitch out.

6 Now begins the stitch-n-flip section of this design. Refer to the fabric placement chart on page 47 for the stitching order. Start your machine and allow a placement line to stitch.

7 Pick up a 3" fabric triangle and place it right side down along the placement line. Ensure that the triangle extends at least ¼" beyond both ends of the placement line. Start your machine and allow the tacking line to stitch.

8 Using curved scissors, trim away the excess fabric, trimming right up to the tacking line. Slide the pressing pad under the hoop, flip back the triangle and fuse it into place using the mini iron. Remove the pressing pad.

NOTES FROM NANCY

If you don't have a mini iron, remove the hoop from the machine and use a small hobby iron and pressing pad. Remember: *Release the hoop, but never the fabric!*

9 Repeat this process until all nine pieces have been placed. Follow the fabric placement chart for the sequence.

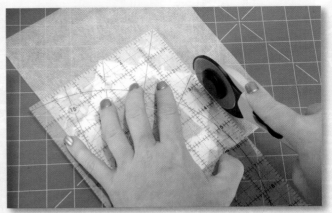

10 Remove the finished block from the hoop. Square up the block, making sure to leave ¼" around the large reference square. Stitch out the designs on the remaining blocks.

11 Determine the arrangement of the blocks. Pin W and E together, right sides facing.

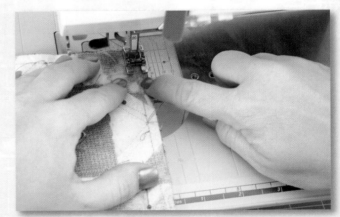

12 Sew along the lines of the original reference square. Press the seams open.

13 Repeat this process with the remaining blocks until all the blocks are attached.

14 Pin a 3½" side border along one side, right sides together, aligning the edges. The border should extend past the top and bottom edges of the banner (we'll trim this later).

15 Sew the border to the banner, leaving a ¼" seam allowance. Press back. Repeat Steps 14 and 15 for the other side.

16 Trim away the excess fabric, using the top and bottom edges of the banner as a guide.

17 Pin the top border to the banner, right sides together, aligning the edges with a little overhang on each side. Sew together, leaving a ¼" seam allowance.

18 Trim off the excess fabric, using the edges of the banner as a guide. Press back.

19 Cut the 12½" square in half diagonally to create two triangles.

20 Locate the center of the triangle's base by folding it in half. Crease the halfway point with the mini-iron.

21 Align the creased center point of the triangle with the bottom point of the last block's diamond.

22 Flip the triangle and pin it to the bottom of the banner, aligning the edges and keeping the right sides and centers together.

23 Sew together, and then press back.

24 Using the sides of the banner as a guide, trim off the triangle's corners.

25 Lay the large piece of batting down, then place the banner on top, using temporary spray adhesive between the two layers. If you prefer, you can use pins to keep both from shifting. Stitch down the seams to secure the batting to the top. Trim the excess batting away.

26 Tape one end of the ribbon in place at the top-left corner, about ½" from the left edge of the banner. Do the same on the right side. Allow each ribbon end to extend beyond the edge of the fabric about 1". Make sure the ribbon is completely inside the banner's edges; bunch it up and tape it securely in place.

27 Position the 14" × 49" backing rectangle right side down on the pressing pad. Fold top down 4" and press. You should now have a 14" × 45" fabric rectangle. Place this right side down on top of the welcome banner, with the folded edge approximately 2½" from top of the banner. Make sure the lower half of the banner is covered.

28 Place the remaining 5" × 14" piece of backing fabric right side down, overlapping the fold by at least 3" and making sure that the top remaining portion is also covered.

29 Carefully flip the banner over and pin all layers in place from the batting side.

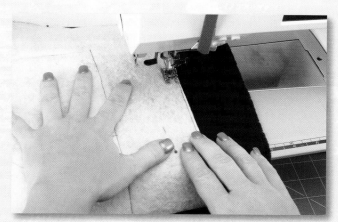

30 Stitch all around the banner, ¼" from the edge. Remove the pins and trim off the excess fabric.

31 Turn the banner inside out, using a point turner for neat corners. Press the banner. Stitch ¼" all around the banner to give it a nice finished edge.

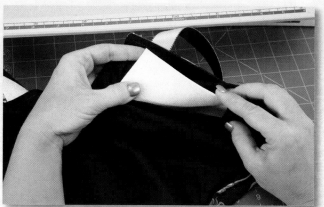

32 Insert Timtex under the inner lip of the backing. This adds stiffness so the banner will hang neatly.

Pillow with Fleur-de-Lys Appliqué

Combining techniques always adds a new dimension to any project. We're going to stitch a pillow that is elegant, yet functional enough to use in any room of the house. Not only will we be piecing, we will learn how to appliqué.

14" × 14"

FABRIC & THREAD

FABRIC FOR BLOCKS

One 3" square for the center

Two 3" squares, cut diagonally to make the four inner triangles

Two 3¾" squares, cut diagonally to make the four outer triangles

FABRIC FOR APPLIQUÉ BLOCKS

Two 5" squares for the background

Two 4" squares

Two 3" squares

Two 2" squares

FABRIC FOR BACKING

One 16" square

One 12" × 16" rectangle

FABRIC FOR BORDERS

Two 1" × 9" maroon strips

Two 1" × 10" maroon strips

Two 1½" ×10" blue strips

Two 1⅓" × 13" blue strips

Two 2" × 13" green strips

Two 2" × 17" green strips

BATTING

One 16" square

THREAD

Embroidery thread for the appliqué

Neutral cotton thread for piecing

EMBROIDERY DESIGN

econpillow1

econpillow2

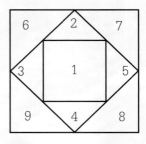

ECONOMY PATCH FABRIC
PLACEMENT CHART

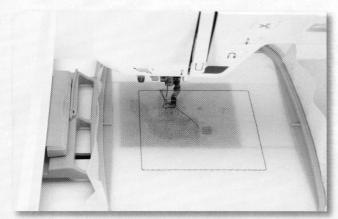

1 Load the first design (econpillow1). Thread the machine. Hoop the stabilizer. Start the machine and allow the large reference square to stitch.

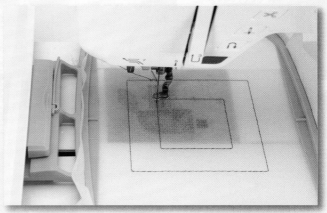

2 Start the machine and allow the small placement line square to stitch.

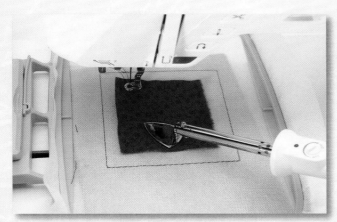

3 Place the 3" fabric square for the center over the placement square, right side up. Make sure the entire small square is covered. Slip a pressing pad under the hoop, and using a mini iron, fuse the center square in place.

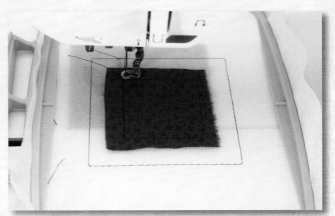

4 Start the machine and the same square will stitch, tacking down the center square.

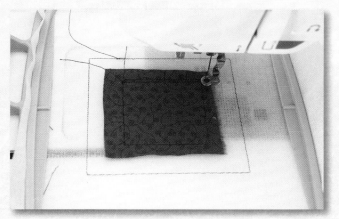

5 Now begins the stitch-n-flip section of this design. Refer to the fabric placement chart on page 56 for the stitching order. Start your machine and allow a placement line to stitch.

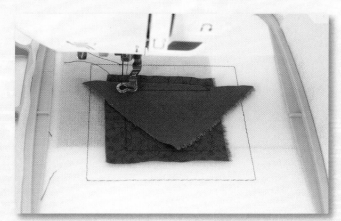

6 Grab an inside corner fabric triangle and place it right side down along the placement line. Ensure that the fabric triangle extends at least ¼" beyond both ends of the placement line. Start your machine and allow the tacking line to stitch. Trim away the excess fabric.

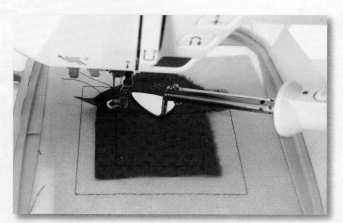

7 Slip a pressing pad under the hoop. Use the mini iron to press the fabric back, fusing it in place. Remove the pressing pad.

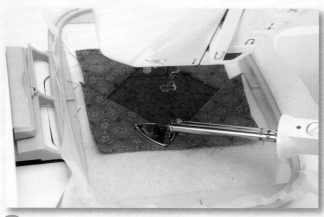

8 Repeat this process until all nine pieces have been placed. Refer to the fabric placement chart for the sequence.

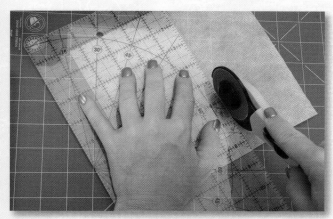

9 Remove the block from the hoop. Turn the block upside down and locate the original reference square. Using a quilter's ruler and a rotary cutter, trim ¼" outside all sides of this square.

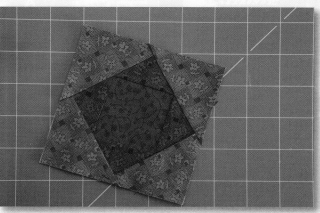

10 Repeat Steps 1–9 to create a second Economy Patch block. To create the appliqué blocks, load the second design (econpillow2). Thread the machine with coordinating embroidery thread. Hoop the stabilizer. Start the machine and allow the large reference square to stitch.

11 Remove the hoop from the machine and place it on a pressing pad. Position a 5" background square, right side up, over the reference square. Use a mini iron to fuse it in place, making sure the reference square is covered.

12 Return the hoop to the machine. Allow the fleur-de-lys placement design to stitch out.

13 Position the 4" fabric square right side up over the fleur-de-lys placement design. Start the machine and allow the fleur-de-lys design to stitch out again, tacking the fabric down (tacking line). Remove the hoop from the machine.

14 Trim away the excess fabric, trimming right next to the tacking line. Be careful not to clip any threads.

15 Return the hoop to the machine. Start the machine and allow the satin stitch to run.

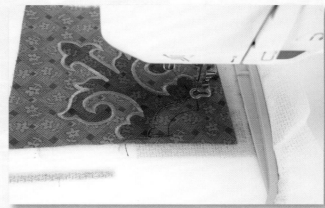

16 When the satin stitching is complete, allow the machine to stitch out the next placement line for the fleur-de-lys design. You may change the thread color to match the next two fabric pieces if you prefer.

NOTES FROM **NANCY**

Instead of making an appliqué, you can stitch the fleur-de-lys design directly on the fabric. This time-honored motif is very distinctive; the outline and satin stitches are beautiful with or without a contrasting appliqué fabric.

17 Position a 3" fabric square right side up over the area that just stitched out. Start the machine and allow the tacking line to stitch.

18 Remove the hoop from the machine and trim right next to the stitched line. Be careful not to clip any threads.

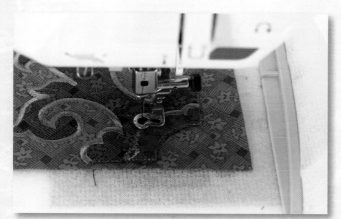

19 Return the hoop to the machine and allow the satin stitch to run.

20 Start the machine and allow the reference line for the next appliqué section to stitch out.

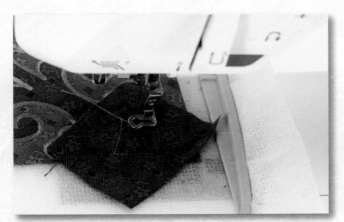

21 Position a 2" fabric square right side up over the area that just stitched out. Start the machine and allow the tacking line to stitch.

22 Remove the hoop from the machine and trim right next to the stitched line. Be careful not to clip any threads.

23 Return the hoop to the machine and allow the satin stitch to run.

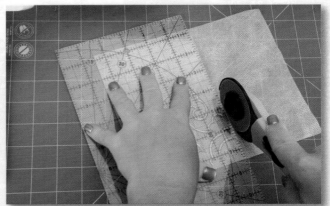

24 Once the appliqué portion is complete, remove the block from the hoop, flip it over and trim ¼" from the edges of the reference square. Repeat Steps 10–24 to create a second appliqué block.

Putting the Project Together

When you're ready to put the pillow together, switch to your sewing machine. Refer to the photo on page 56 for the arrangement. Sew each Economy Patch block to an appliqué block, then stitch the rows together.

Next, sew on the borders starting with the 1" strips, and building to the 2" strips (maroon, blue then green).

For the backing, take the 16" square and fold one edge back 4". Place this right side down on the pillow top, about 4" from the top. Press the fold to crease.

Next, take the 10" × 16" rectangle and fold one longer edge back 4". Press. Place it right side down on the right side of the pillow top, with the folded edge facing toward the center. Overlap the other folded edge by 3". Stitch around the outside edge. Turn inside out and neatly press. Insert a pillow form or fill with craft pillow stuffing.

Miniature Quilt

There's nothing cuter on little quilts than little hearts. This one features both pieced and appliquéd hearts. There are several ways that you can display little quilts of this type. You can create a sleeve and stitch it to the back, or you could attach ribbon tabs to hang the quilt from a decorative rod. Tabs can easily be made from coordinating fabrics, too.

15" × 15"

FABRIC & THREAD

FABRIC FOR PIECED BLOCKS
One 1½" × 2" rectangle
Three 1½" squares
Three 1" × 3¼" rectangles
Two 1½" × 2½" rectangles

FABRIC FOR APPLIQUÉD BLOCKS
One 5" square
One 4" square

FABRIC FOR BORDERS
Two 2½" × 12" strips
Two 2½" × 17" strips

FABRIC FOR SASHING
Six 1" × 3½" strips
Two 1" × 12" strips

FABRIC FOR BACKING
One 17" square

BATTING
One 17" square

THREAD
Neutral thread for piecing
Thread for satin stitching

EMBROIDERY DESIGN
heartmini1
heartmini2

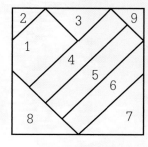

HEART FABRIC
PLACEMENT CHART

63

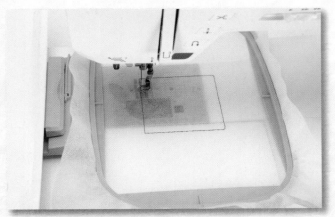

1 Load your designs (heartmini1 and heartmini2). Pull up the appropriate design (heartmini1). Thread the machine and hoop the stabilizer. Start the machine and allow the reference line square to stitch.

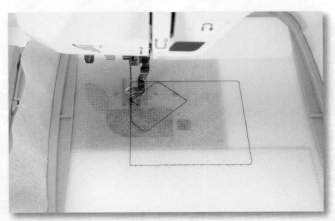

2 Start the machine and allow the placement shape to stitch.

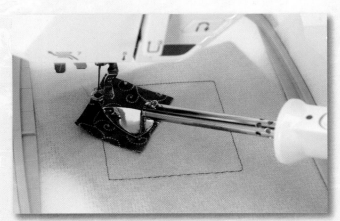

3 Place the 1½" × 2½" rectangle right side up over the placement shape. Make sure it covers the entire stitched shape. Slip a pressing pad under the hoop, then fuse the fabric in place using a mini iron. Remove the pressing pad.

4 Now begins the stitch-n-flip section of the project. Start the machine and allow a placement line to stitch.

5 Grab a 1½" square and place it right side down along the placement line. Ensure that the square extends at least ¼" beyond both ends of the line. Start the machine and allow a tacking line to stitch.

Trim the excess fabric right up to the tacking line. Slip a pressing pad under the hoop, flip the fabric back and fuse it in place using a mini iron. Remove the pressing pad.

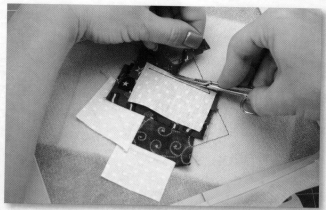

6 Repeat this process until all nine pieces are in place. Refer to the fabric placement chart on page 63 for the stitching order. Make sure to trim as you go, especially with this type of block; many layers of fabric can quickly lead to bulky seams. Stitch a total of four pieced blocks.

7 Square up all four blocks by trimming ¼" outside the reference line square.

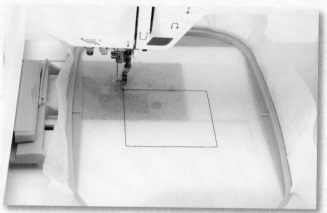

8 Once you have completed all four pieced hearts, it's time to create the appliquéd heart blocks. Pull up the appropriate design (heartmini2) and thread the machine with the embroidery thread. Hoop the stabilizer. Start the machine and allow the reference line square to stitch.

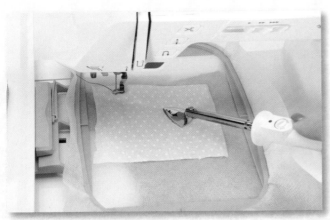

9 Place the 5" square right-side up over the reference line square. Slip a pressing pad under the hoop and, using your mini iron, fuse the fabric in place. Remove the pressing pad.

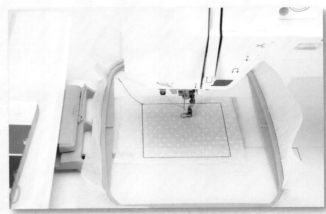

10 Start the machine and allow the tacking line to stitch. This will secure the fabric completely. Sometimes, when stitching appliqué designs, the fabric gets tugged in or can shift. You can avoid that by stitching this extra tacking line.

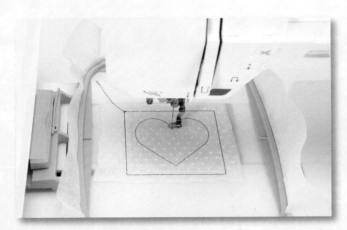

11 Once the fabric is tacked down, start the machine and allow the placement shape to run.

12 Place the heart fabric right side up over the placement shape. Make sure it covers the entire heart shape. Start the machine and allow the tacking line to stitch. Remove the hoop from the machine. Using your curved scissors, trim as close to the tacking line as possible.

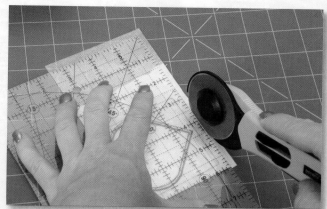

13 Return the hoop to the machine. You can change embroidery threads to match your fabrics. Start the machine and allow the satin stitch to run.
Create five appliquéd heart blocks.

14 Square up your appliquéd hearts by flipping them over and then using a rotary cutter and quilter's ruler to trim ¼" outside the reference line square.

Putting the Project Together

When you're ready to put the quilt top together, switch to your sewing machine. To create the quilt top, sew two rows as follows: appliquéd heart + 1" × 3½" strip + pieced heart + 1" × 3½" strip + appliquéd heart.
Sew one row as follows: pieced heart + 1" × 3½" strip + appliquéd heart + 1" × 3½" strip + pieced heart.
Add the 1" × 12" sashing strips between the rows, making sure the row with the pieced heart in the center is the middle row. Using a quilter's ruler and rotary cutter, square up the top.
Attach the 2½" × 12" side borders, then the top and bottom 2½" × 17" borders. Trim away the excess fabric each time. Finish as desired.

Frame Cover

This design was created to fit a 4" × 6" acrylic standing frame. It will also fit a 4" × 6" magnetic acrylic frame. It is made all in one hooping and is ready to display once complete. The design is versatile; you can use a solid square instead of the heart block in the center, and embroider the cover with your favorite design or saying.

4½" × 6¼"

FABRIC & THREAD

FABRIC FOR BLOCK

One 1¾" × 2½" rectangle

One 2" square

Three 1¼" × 3½" strips

Two 1¼" × 2" rectangles

Two 2" × 3" rectangles

FABRIC FOR BACKGROUND

One 1½" × 3¾" strip

Two 1½" × 4½" strips

One 4¼" × 5¼" strip

FABRIC FOR BACKING

One 5¼" × 8" rectangle

THREAD

Neutral cotton thread for piecing

EMBROIDERY DESIGNS

heartframe

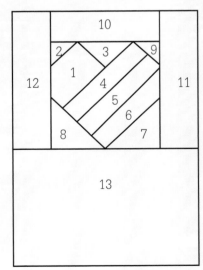

HEART FABRIC
PLACEMENT CHART

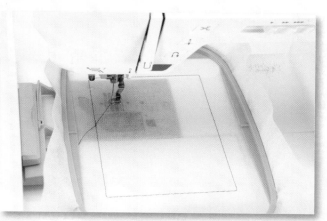

1 Load the design (heartframe) and thread the machine. Hoop the stabilizer. Start the machine and allow the reference line rectangle to stitch.

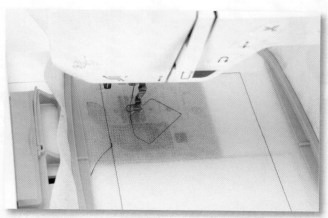

2 Start the machine and allow the placement shape to stitch.

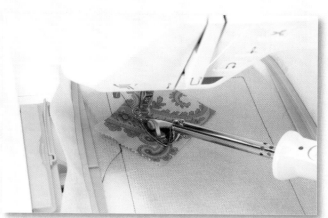

3 Place the 1¾" × 2½" rectangle right-side up over the placement shape. Make sure the placement stitching is covered. Slide a pressing pad under the hoop. Using a mini iron, fuse the fabric in place. Remove the pressing pad.

4 Now begins the stitch-n-flip section of the project. Start the machine and allow a placement line to stitch.

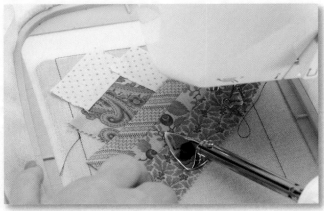

5 Place one of the 1¼" × 2" rectangles right side down along the placement line. Ensure that the rectangle extends at least ¼" beyond both ends of the placement line. Start the machine and allow the tacking line to stitch.

Trim the fabric close to the tacking line with your curved scissors. Slip a pressing pad under the hoop. Flip the fabric back. Using your mini iron, fuse the fabric in place. Remove the pressing pad.

6 Repeat the stitch-n-flip process until the first twelve fabric pieces have been placed. Refer to the fabric placement chart on page 68 for the stitching order.

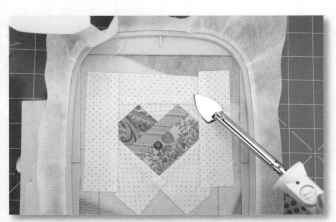

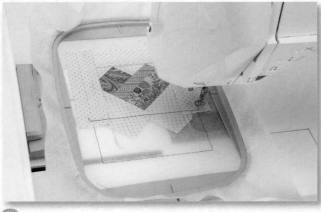

7 Add the top and side borders of the frame cover.

8 Start the machine and allow the placement line to run.

NOTES FROM NANCY

This is an amazing project. You can watch Larisa stitch this Frame Cover on the DVD (click *Heart Block* on the main menu). As you watch this project progress, the folding and placement of the backing fabric seems to be completed almost by magic!

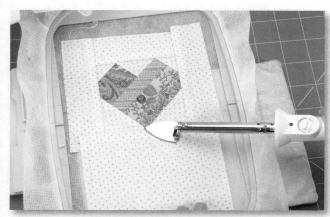

9 Place the 4¼" × 5¼" rectangle right side down along the placement line. Ensure that the rectangle extends at least ¼" beyond both ends of the placement line. Start the machine and allow the tacking line to stitch. Remove the hoop from the machine and trim away the excess fabric. Slip a pressing pad under the hoop. Flip the fabric down and fuse it in place using a mini iron, concentrating the heat toward the seam line.

10 Fold the fabric under, extending the fold a smidgen below the stitched line. Use the mini iron to fuse the fabric in place. This will create a finished edge for your frame cover.

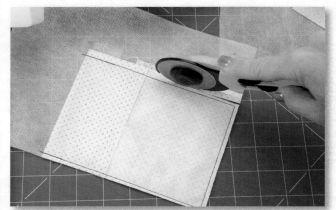

11 Fold back the edge of the backing fabric, wrong sides together, about 1". (Here, my fabric is a little longer than the recommended 5¼" × 8".) Regardless of the length, fold the fabric back just enough so the end of the folded edges align, and so that the fabric still covers the entire design.

12 Return the hoop to the machine. Start the machine and allow the tacking line to stitch. The tacking line will double back along the sides of the fold for reinforcement. Remove the project from the hoop. Using the rotary cutter, trim the excess fabric to ¼" around all sides except the folded edge.

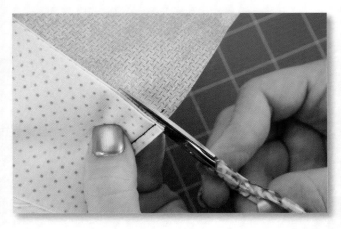

13 Use scissors to trim the stabilizer away from the folded edge.

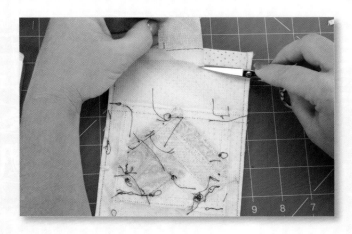

14 Continue trimming away the stabilizer, trimming out a "scoop" from the heart side. Nip the corners to make it easier to turn the project inside out.

15 Turn the project inside out. Use a point turner to push out the corners for nice, clean edges. Neatly press. Slide it on the acrylic frame and it's ready to be displayed.

Kitchen Towel

Here's a remarkable way to show off your quilting skills in the kitchen. This kitchen towel has a ribbon attached so that it can hang from any stove or decorative knob. The heart is pieced, then appliquéd onto the towel. You can stitch the same design on matching accessories such as placemats or kitchen curtains. How about using it to decorate an apron? The possibilities are numerous.

FABRIC & THREAD

FABRIC FOR BLOCK
One 2" × 3" rectangle
Three 2" squares
Three 1½" × 4½" rectangles
Two 2¼" × 4" rectangles

FABRIC FOR TOWEL TOPPER
Two 5½" × 8" rectangles

BATTING
One 6" square

THREAD
Two coordinating embroidery threads
Neutral cotton thread for piecing

OTHER
Hand towel
One 7" square of Solvy
One 24" piece of 1" wide ribbon

EMBROIDERY DESIGNS
hearttowel1
hearttowel2

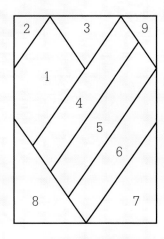

HEART FABRIC
PLACEMENT CHART

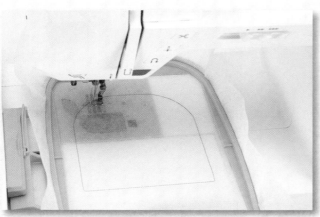

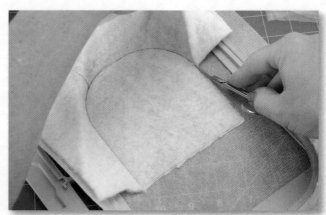

1 Load the design (hearttowel2) and thread the machine using a color that coordinates with your fabric. Hoop the stabilizer. Start the machine and allow a box with a rounded top to stitch. This is your reference shape.

2 Lay the 6" square of batting on top of this shape. Start your machine and allow a tacking line to stitch. Remove the hoop from the machine. Using the curved scissors, trim the excess batting, getting as close to the tacking line as possible.

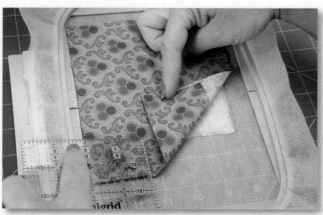

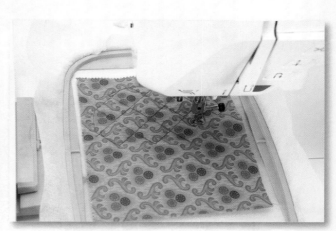

3 Fold one end of one 5½" × 8" rectangle up 2", wrong sides together, and press it. Place it right side up with the folded edge along the straight bottom of the shape. Make sure it overlaps the bottom reference line by about 1½".

4 Start the machine and allow the quilting to take place.

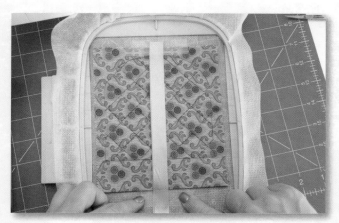

5 Fold the ribbon in half, wrong sides together. Place the folded edge on the rounded end of the towel topper, making sure it extends 1" past the edge. Press and then tape in place. The loose ends of the ribbon should hang toward the bottom of the towel topper. Tape the loose ends in place to keep them from shifting.

6 Fold the end of the other 5½" × 8" rectangle up 2", wrong sides together, and press it. Place it right side down with the folded edge next to the folded edge of the first rectangle.

7 Tape the fabric in place, especially along the fold, so it will not get caught up in the foot once the final stitching begins.

8 Start the machine and allow the final tacking line to stitch. The tacking line will double back over the edges of the folds and at the ribbon for reinforcement. Remove the project from the hoop, Using a rotary cutter, trim ¼" away from the tacking line.

9 Use your scissors to trim a "scoop" out of the stabilizer from the open end of the towel topper. Be careful not to cut the ribbon.

10 Turn inside out. Use the opposite end of the point turner to smooth out the curve. Press the towel topper from the back; this will help preserve the loft of the batting.

11 Pull up the next design (hearttowel2) on the machine. Thread the machine and hoop the stabilizer. Determine where you would like the design to appear on the towel. Place this area at the center of the hoop. To preserve the loft of the towel, don't iron it in place. Instead, use adhesive spray or carefully pin it to the stabilizer.

12 Start the machine and allow the reference line shape stitch. This shows the overall outline of the project. It's difficult to see here; the thread can get a little lost in the loft of the towel.

NOTES FROM **NANCY**

Lay the towel flat (not bunched or folded) to make certain it doesn't catch under the hoop.

76

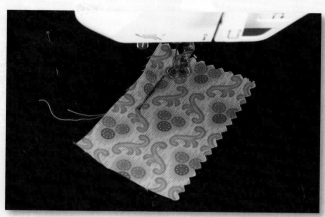

13 Start the machine and allow the placement line shape to stitch.

14 Place the first piece of fabric right side up over the placement line shape. Make sure the entire shape is covered. Start your machine and allow a placement line to stitch.

15 Now begins the stitch-n-flip section of this design. Please refer to the fabric placement chart on page 73 for the stitching order. Place the second piece of fabric right side down along the placement line. Ensure that the fabric extends at least ¼" beyond both ends of the placement line. Start the machine and allow a tacking line to stitch.

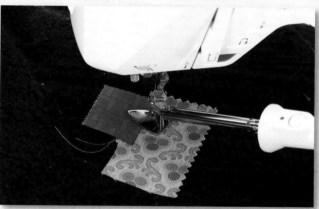

16 Slip a pressing pad under the hoop, flip piece 2 back, and press. It won't fuse in place, but if you concentrate the heat along the seam, it should stay neatly in place.

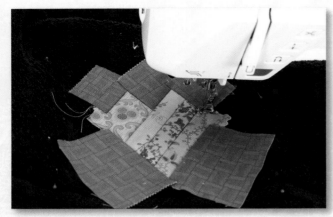

17 Repeat this process until all nine pieces have been placed.

18 Now that the heart has been pieced we will finish off the edges using a satin stitch. If you need to change thread to coordinate with the heart, do so now. Start the machine and allow a tacking line to stitch.

19 Trim away the excess fabric as close to the tacking line as possible. You don't want stray bits of fabric peeking through the satin stitch.

20 Use a lint roller to remove all the stray threads and bits of fabric.

21 If you're using a terry towel or something similar, I recommend that you lay a water-soluble stabilizer on top of your design before satin stitching. This will prevent the satin stitches from becoming buried in the towel, and will produce a much nicer stitched line. Start the machine and allow the satin stitches to run.

22 Remove the project from the hoop. Tear away the stabilizer from around the outside of the rectangle.

NOTES FROM **NANCY**

If you still have a few remnants of the water-soluble stabilizer caught in the stitching, spritz them with a water bottle. Presto, they will disappear!

23 Using the sharp tip of your curved scissors, pick up the corner of the stabilizer on the inside of the rectangle, and then tear away.

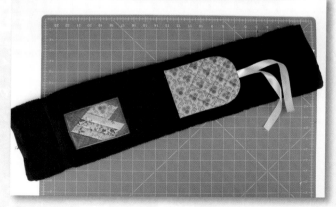

24 Fold the towel and lay it out so the design is in the center. Determine the placement of the towel topper.

25 Once you've determined the placement, determine where you will need to cut. The towel will need to extend into the topper past the bottom stitched line.

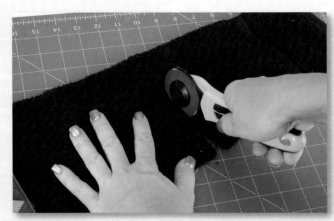

26 Use your rotary cutter to cut straight across the towel at your determined point.

27 Without shifting the folds too much, bunch up the towel across the raw edge, and slide it into the towel topper.

28 Sew the towel in place. Straight stitch right across the bottom quilting line. Your towel is now ready to hang!

Pillow with Rooster Appliqué

By now you've already learned how to piece a block and how to appliqué, so why not appliqué onto a block? We'll start with a Log Cabin block, add sashing, cornerstones and borders, then we'll add a new dimension by appliquéing a cute rooster to a corner. With these techniques, you can make full-sized quilts, lap quilts or wall hangings.

11½" × 11½"

FABRIC & THREAD

FABRIC FOR BLOCKS
One 1¾" square for the center

Twelve scraps for the logs, 1" wide and up to 6" long

FABRIC FOR APPLIQUÉ
One green 3" square

One red 3" × 4" rectangle

One brown 3" × 3½" rectangle

One yellow 2" × 2½" rectangle

FABRIC FOR SASHING
Four 3½" × 5½" strips

Four 3½" squares for the cornerstones

FABRIC FOR BORDERS
Two 1" × 12½" strips

Two 1" × 14" strips

FABRIC FOR BACKING
Two 10" × 13" rectangles

BATTING
One 13" square

THREAD
Embroidery threads for design (orange, green, brown, red, yellow and black)

Neutral cotton thread for piecing

EMBROIDERY DESIGNS
logcabnpill1

logcabnpill2

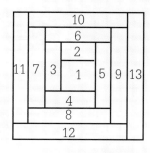

LOG CABIN FABRIC
PLACEMENT CHART

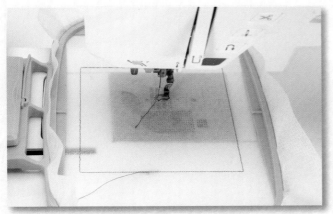

1 Load the designs. Pull up the first design (logcabnpill1) and thread the machine with thread for piecing. A neutral color is best; I've used black thread here for visibility. Hoop the stabilizer and put the hoop on the machine. Start the machine and allow the reference square to stitch.

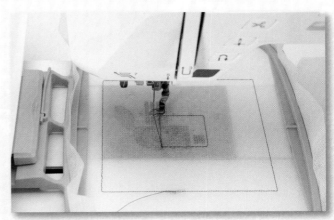

2 Start the machine and allow the placement shape to stitch.

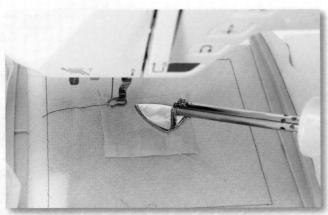

3 Place the center square right side up over the placement shape, making sure the fabric covers the entire shape. Slip a pressing pad under the hoop. Using the mini iron, fuse the fabric in place. Remove the pressing pad.

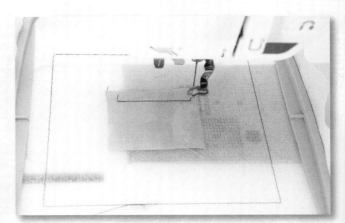

4 Start the machine and allow a placement line to stitch.

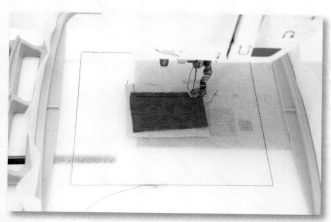

5 Place piece 2 right side down along the placement line. Ensure that piece 2 extends at least ¼" beyond both ends of the placement line. Start the machine and allow a tacking line to stitch.

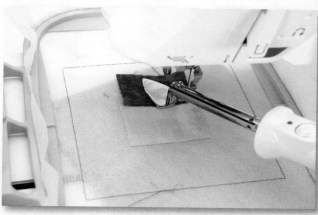

6 Slip a pressing pad under the hoop. Flip the fabric back and, using your mini iron, fuse the fabric in place. Remove the pressing pad.

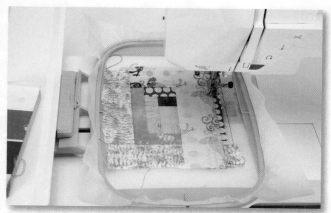

7 Repeat this process until all thirteen fabrics have been placed. Refer to the fabric placement chart on page 81 to help you lay out the pieces.

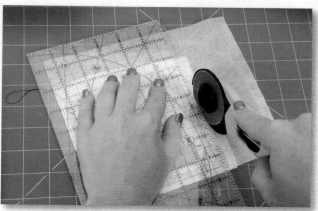

8 Remove the finished block from the hoop. To square up the block, flip to the back and use a rotary cutter and quilter's ruler to trim ¼" outside the reference square.

Refer to the fabric placement chart on page 81

NOTES FROM **NANCY**

Assembling the pieces can be tricky with the Log Cabin block. To help with this, cut all your pieces in advance, and lay them out in order according to the placement chart. Then you can just grab and go!

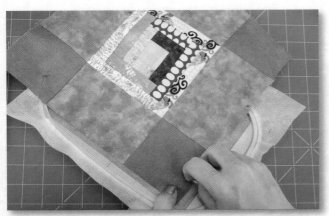

9 Stitch one 3½" × 5½" rectangle to top and bottom of the block. Stitch a 3½" cornerstone to each end of the two other 3½" × 5½" rectangles, then stitch them to the sides of the block, as shown in the photo. Hoop the stabilizer. Determine where you want your rooster appliqué to go. Center that area in the hoop, and then fuse to the stabilizer. Add pins for extra stability and security.

10 Pull up the next design (logcabnpill2). Thread the machine with orange embroidery thread. I used this color until it was time for all the satin stitching. Start the machine and let the beak and feet stitch out.

11 Using the same thread color, start the machine and allow the placement shape for the tail feathers to stitch out.

12 Place a piece of red fabric right side up over the placement shape for the tail feathers. Make sure the shape is completely covered. Start the machine and allow the tacking line to stitch.

NOTES FROM **NANCY**

If you decide to appliqué the rooster on the Log Cabin block, keep in mind that you'll be stitching over several layers of fabric. To prevent the needle from breaking, consider changing to a slightly larger needle and/or setting your machine to a slower stitching speed.

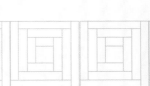

13 Remove the hoop from the machine. Using the curved scissors, trim as close to the tacking line as you can.

14 Return the hoop to the machine. Start the machine and allow the placement shape for the rooster's body to stitch.

15 Place a piece of brown fabric right side up over the placement shape for the rooster's body. Make sure the shape is completely covered. Start the machine and allow the tacking line to stitch.

Remove the hoop from the machine. Using the curved scissors, trim as close to the tacking line as you can.

16 Return the hoop to the machine. Start the machine and allow the placement shape for the wing to stitch.

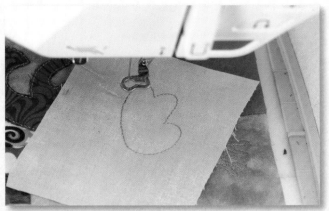

17 Place a piece of yellow fabric right side up over the placement shape for the wing. Make sure the shape is completely covered. Start the machine and allow the tacking line to stitch.

Remove the hoop from the machine. Using the curved scissors, trim as close to the tacking line as you can.

18 Return the hoop to the machine. Start the machine and allow the placement shape for the neck to stitch.

19 Place a piece of green fabric right side up over the placement shape for the neck. Make sure the shape is completely covered. Start the machine and allow the tacking line to stitch.

Remove the hoop from the machine. Using the curved scissors, trim as close to the tacking line as you can.

20 Now begins the satin stitching, so thread the machine with red. Return the hoop to the machine. Start the machine and allow the satin stitching to run.

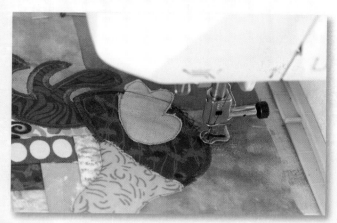

21 Thread the machine with brown. Start the machine to continue the satin stitching.

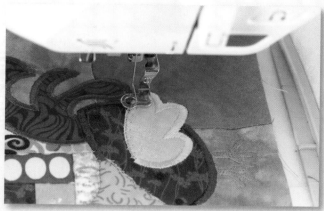

22 Thread the machine with yellow. Start the machine to continue the satin stitching.

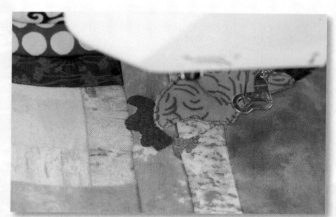

23 Thread the machine with red. Start the machine and allow the rooster's comb to stitch.

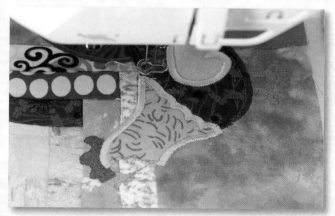

24 Thread the machine with green. Start the machine to continue the satin stitching.

25 Thread the machine with red. Start the machine and allow the rooster's wattle to stitch.

26 Finally, change the thread to black. Start the machine and allow the eye to stitch.

Putting the Project Together

For the pillow, sew the top and bottom borders to the block. Square up using a rotary cutter and quilter's ruler. Sew the cornerstones to the side borders, and then sew to the pillow top. Square up using a quilter's ruler and rotary cutter. We have the pillow top completed, so all we need to do now is add a 13" × 13" layer of batting. Stitch down the block seams to give a quilted effect to the pillow. Trim the excess batting. To create the sham-style backing, take the two 10" × 13" pieces of backing fabric and fold one edge of each down 3". Each will now measure 7" × 13". Place one of the folded 7" × 13" rectangles with the fold on top and position it about 2" above the center, right side down. Place the other 7" × 13" rectangle, right side down, with the top folded edge pointing down over the first. Make sure that the entire pillow top is covered. Gently turn it over and pin in place. Leaving a ¼" seam allowance, stitch all around the pillow top. Turn it inside out, use the point turner on the corners, then neatly press using a pressing cloth. Stuff the pillow with fiberfill.

Itty Bitty Ornament

How fun is it to know that you can create miniature quilt blocks with such precision? Not only will this project make a gift any quilting friend would be happy to receive for Christmas, it can also be displayed year round. Try adding a clasp pin to the back so that you can wear it to your next guild meeting. Your ornament is now wearable art.

2" × 2"

FABRIC & THREAD

FABRIC FOR BLOCKS

Twelve scraps for the logs, ½" wide and up to 3" long

One 1" square for the center

FABRIC FOR BACKING

Two 2½" squares

OTHER

One 6" piece of ⅛" wide ribbon

THREAD

Neutral cotton thread for piecing

EMBROIDERY DESIGNS

logcabnorn

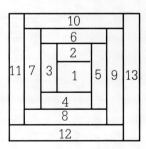

LOG CABIN FABRIC
PLACEMENT CHART

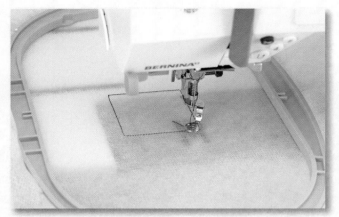

1 Load the design (logcabnorn) and thread the machine. Hoop the stabilizer. Start the machine and allow the reference line square to stitch.

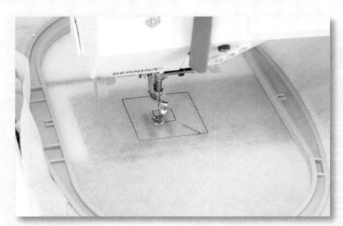

2 Start the machine and allow the placement square to stitch.

3 Place the center square fabric right side up over the placement square. Make sure it completely covers the square. Slip a pressing pad under the hoop and use the mini iron to fuse the fabric in place. Remove the pressing pad.

4 Start the machine and allow the placement line to stitch.

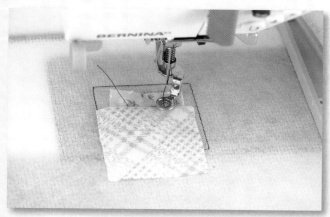

5 Now begins the stitch-n-flip section of the design. Place piece 2 right side down along the placement line. Ensure that piece 2 extends at least ¼" beyond both ends of the placement line. ⅛

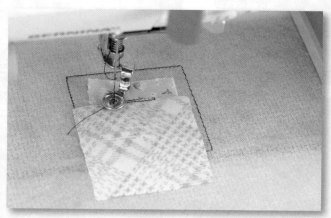

6 Start the machine and allow the tacking line to stitch. The tacking line will stitch very close to the edge of piece 2.

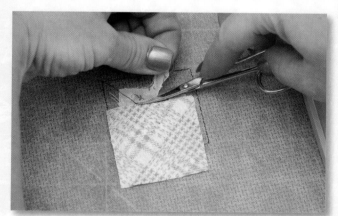

7 Remove the hoop from the machine. Using the curved scissors, trim away the excess fabric.

8 Slip a pressing pad under the hoop. Flip the fabric back and use the mini iron to fuse the fabric in place.

9 Place the hoop back on the machine. Repeat this process until all thirteen pieces are in place.

10 Loop the ribbon and position it either at a corner or in the center of one side (depending on how you want the ornament to hang). Place so that the raw edges point toward the edge of the block and the loop hangs in the middle. Tape in place. (Make sure the loop is tucked inside the reference line square; flip the hoop over to check if necessary.)

11 Fold one of the 2½" square backing pieces back by about ½", wrong sides together. Crease the fold with the mini iron. Position this over the block so the fold is at the middle.

12 Fold the other 2½" square backing piece and crease as in Step 11. Lay this over the previous backing piece as shown, and tape in place.

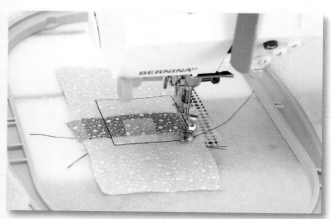

13 Return the hoop to the machine. Start the machine and allow a tacking square to stitch, securing the ribbon and backing pieces.

14 Remove the project from the hoop. Using a rotary cutter, trim 1/8" outside the tacking square.

15 Remove the tape as needed and turn it inside out. Use a point turner for neat corners. Press neatly. It's ready to hang.

Create a Log Cabin brooch in minutes! Refer to the *Itty Bitty Ornament* project and just omit the ribbons. When you've finished stitching the block, glue or hand-stitch a pin back to the underside of the brooch. It's a clever accessory!

NOTES FROM **NANCY**

Quilt Label

What better way to sign your quilted work than with a custom-made quilt label? After the piecing is finished, you can use the text provided or create your own. You can even make a money or gift card pouch from this design by using the sham-style backing that you have already learned to sew. My cousin Grammie Tammie suggested using the pouch to store scrap pieces of fabric that go with the top. Stitch it to the back of the quilt. As the years go by and the quilt gets washed repeatedly, the scrap colors will fade with the quilt, thus making the scraps match the top. If your quilt ever gets a tear or a hole in it, remove the pouch and use the enclosed scraps to repair it.

3¾" × 7"

FABRIC & THREAD

FABRIC FOR BLOCKS
One 1¼" square for the center
Twelve scraps for the logs, ¾" wide and up to 3½" long

FABRIC FOR BORDERS
Three 1" × 4½" strips
One 5" square

FABRIC FOR BACKING
One 4½" × 8" rectangle

THREAD
Neutral thread for piecing
Embroidery thread for the design

EMBROIDERY DESIGNS
logcabnlabel

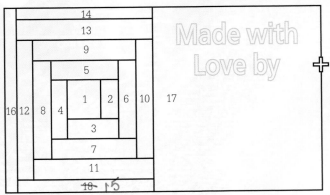

LOG CABIN FABRIC
PLACEMENT CHART

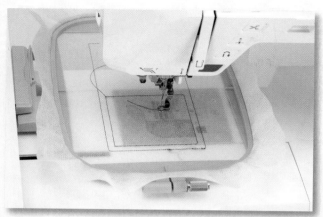

1 Load the design on the machine. Thread the machine with neutral thread. Hoop the stabilizer. Start the machine and allow both the rectangle and square to stitch. The rectangle will be the reference shape for the whole label. The square will be the reference line square for the Log Cabin block.

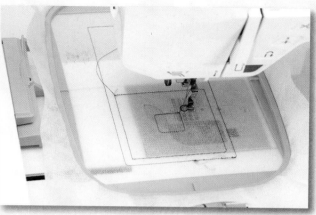

2 Start the machine and allow the placement square to stitch.

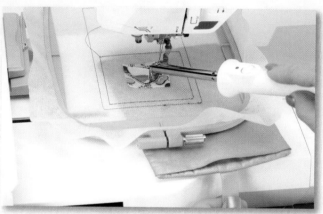

3 Place piece 1 right side up over the placement square. Make sure the fabric covers the square completely. Slip a pressing pad under the hoop and use the mini iron to fuse the fabric in place. Remove the pressing pad.

4 Start the machine and allow a placement line to stitch.

5 Now begins the stitch-n-flip section of the design. Place piece 2 right side down along the placement line. Ensure that piece 2 extends at least ¼" beyond both ends of the placement line. Start the machine and allow the tacking line to stitch. Trim away the excess fabric.

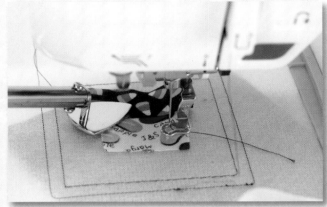

6 Slip a pressing pad under the hoop. Flip piece 2 back and use the mini iron to fuse it into place. Remove the pressing pad.

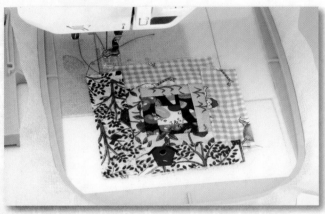

7 Repeat the process until you've placed the thirteen pieces of the Log Cabin block. Refer to the fabric placement chart on page 94 for the sequence.

8 Add the borders by starting the machine and allowing the placement line to stitch. Place top border right side down along the placement line. Start the machine and allow the tacking line to stitch.

Slip a pressing pad under the hoop. Flip top border back and use the mini iron to fuse it into place. Remove the pressing pad.

NOTES FROM **NANCY**

Don't forget to create the Pressing Pad on page 37. The pad and mini iron make a terrific pressing combo to use when piecing in the hoop.

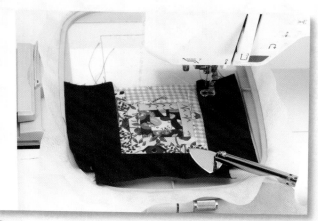

9 Repeat the process for the bottom and left side border pieces. Make sure all pieces extend past the reference shape line.

10 For the large square, allow the machine to stitch out the final placement line. Place the final border piece right side down along the placement line. Start the machine and allow the tacking line to stitch. Remove the hoop from the machine, place it on a pressing pad, flip back the final border piece and fuse it into place with the mini iron.

11 Now that the piecing has finished, you can either use the text provided or create your own. If you use the text provided, program in your own name and date using the text feature on your embroidery machine.

12 Take the 4½" × 8" backing fabric and snip the center. We'll use this hole to turn the project inside out.

13 Place the backing piece over the entire project in the hoop. Start the machine and let a tacking line rectangle stitch.

14 Remove the project from the hoop and trim ¼" outside the tacking line rectangle. Nip the corners.

15 Turn the project inside out through the hole in the backing, using a point turner for the corners. Place the project right side down on the pressing pad and neatly press with the mini iron.

17 Trim away any excess backing. Attach the label to your quilt by hand stitching, or with a fusible adhesive.

Candle Placemat

This placemat is designed to coordinate with the *Candle Covers* project on page 121, but you could easily stitch a set to use for an attractive table setting. Many types of placemats are available for purchase that would work well for this project.

The Pineapple appliqué design shown here may be applied to a variety of items. On the video, you can see that Nancy and I used the Pineapple design in place of the Heart on the Kitchen Towel (page 73).

FABRIC & THREAD

FABRIC FOR BLOCK

One 2½" square for the center

Twelve solid-color scraps, 1" wide and up to 3" long

Four pairs of coordinating scraps, 1" wide and up to 3" long

THREAD

Neutral thread for piecing

Embroidery thread for satin stitching

OTHER

Purchased placemat

EMBROIDERY DESIGNS

pinemat

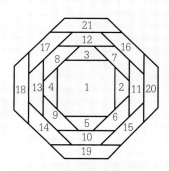

PINEAPPLE PLACEMAT
FABRIC PLACEMENT CHART

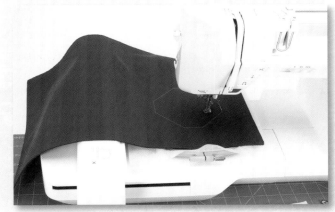

1 Load the design (pinemat) onto the machine. Thread the machine with embroidery thread. Hoop the stabilizer. Determine where you would like to position the block on your placemat. Iron the mat onto the fusible stabilizer in the appropriate place.

2 Place the hoop onto the machine. Start the machine and allow the reference shape to stitch (an octagon).

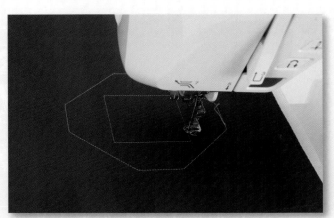

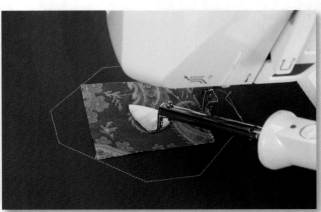

3 Start the machine and allow the placement square to stitch.

4 Place the 2½" square for the center fabric right side up over the placement square. Make sure the entire small square is covered. You may spray the back of the fabric with a temporary adhesive spray before placing it in position if you like. (If you use adhesive, spray it away from the machine.)

NOTES FROM NANCY

To pin a pre-made placemat (or other ready-made projects) to the stabilizer, I use double-sided basting tape. The tape is very tacky and will hold even heavier fabrics in place. Immediately after embroidering, remove the tape. It's easier to remove the tape immediately than waiting until another time!

5 Now begins the stitch-n-flip section of the design. Start the machine and allow the tacking line to stitch. Remove the hoop from the machine and, using the curved scissors, trim away the excess fabric, getting as close to the tacking line as possible. I included this step in case you want to add a monogram or other embroidery design.

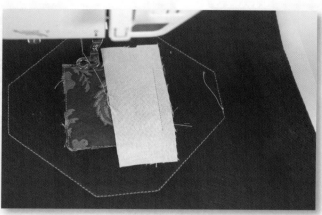

6 Return the hoop to the machine. Start the machine and allow a placement line to stitch. Place piece 2 right side down along the placement line. Ensure that piece 2 extends at least ¼" beyond both ends of the placement line. Start the machine and allow the tacking line to stitch.

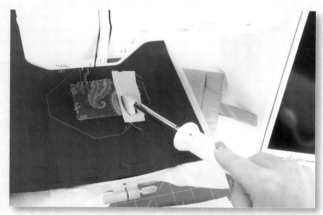

7 Slip a pressing pad under the hoop and press the fabric back using the mini iron. Remove the pressing pad.

8 Continue the stitch-n-flip process, referring to the fabric placement chart on page 99, until all twenty-one pieces have been placed.

9 Start the machine to allow a tacking line to stitch. Remove the hoop from the machine. Trim away the excess fabric as close to the tacking line as possible.

10 Use a lint roller to pick up any stray thread and bits of fabric.

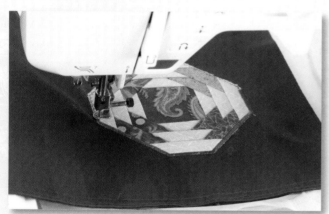

11 Return the hoop to the machine. Allow the satin stitching to run.

12 When the satin stitching is complete, remove the project from the hoop. Flip the placemat over and trim away the stabilizer.

Pincushion

Two things I love are 1930s reproduction fabrics and getting homemade gifts! I've combined my two loves in this quick-stitch project. This pincushion would make a nice gift for any stitcher.

As a bonus idea, you could add ribbon like we did with the *Quilter's Pouch* (see page 42) to make a hanging ornament. Fiberfill stuffing will give it added dimension.

3½" × 3½"

FABRIC & THREAD

FABRIC FOR BLOCK

One 2" square of unbleached muslin

Twelve pink 1" × 3" strips

Two green 1" × 3" strips

Two blue 1" × 3" strips

Two yellow 1" × 3" strips

Two purple 1" × 3" strips

One green 1¾" × 3" piece for the corner

One blue 1¾" × 3" piece for the corner

One yellow 1¾" × 3" piece for the corner

One purple 1¾" × 3" piece for the corner

FABRIC FOR BACKING

Two pink 2½" × 4½" rectangles

THREAD

Neutral thread for piecing

Embroidery thread (gray, pink)

OTHER

Fiberfill or superfine steel wool

EMBROIDERY DESIGNS

pinepincush

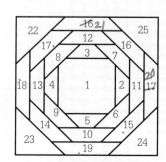

PINEAPPLE PINCUSHION
FABRIC PLACEMENT CHART

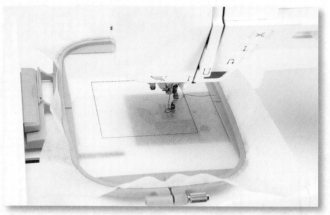

1 Load the design (pinepincush) onto the machine. Thread the machine with the gray embroidery thread. Hoop the stabilizer. Start the machine and allow the reference shape to stitch.

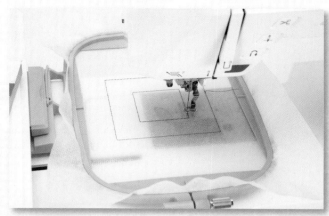

2 Start the machine and allow the placement square to stitch.

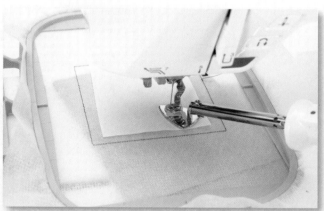

3 Place the muslin square over the placement square, making sure the entire square is covered. (If using fabric with a right and wrong side, place fabric right side up.) Slip a pressing pad under the hoop. Using the mini iron, fuse the fabric in place.

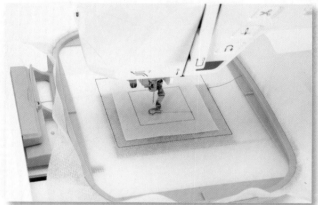

4 Start the machine and allow a tacking line square to stitch, securing the muslin to the stabilizer. This will keep the fabric from puckering when the design is applied.

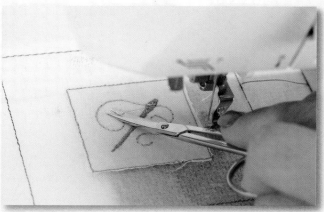

5 Remove the hoop from the machine. Using your curved scissors, trim away the excess fabric, right up to the tacking line square.

6 Return the hoop to the machine. Start the machine and allow the needle design to stitch. Change the thread to pink. Start the machine and allow the thread part of the design to stitch.

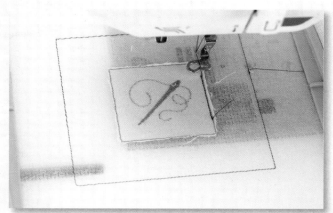

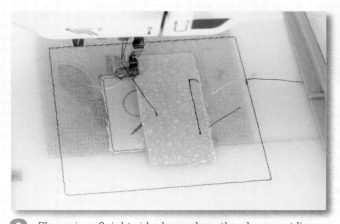

7 Now begins the stitch-n-flip section of this design. Please refer to the fabric placement chart on page 103 for the stitching order. Change the thread to neutral. (I've used black thread for visibility.) Start the machine and allow a placement line to stitch.

8 Place piece 2 right side down along the placement line. Ensure that piece 2 extends at least ¼" beyond both ends of the placement line. Start the machine and allow the tacking line to stitch.

Slip a pressing pad under the hoop. Flip the fabric back and fuse it in place with the mini iron.

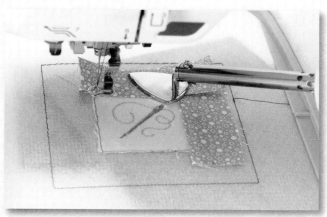

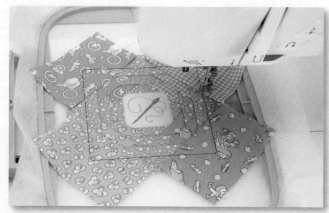

9 Start the machine and allow a placement line to stitch. Place piece 3 right side down along the placement line. Ensure that piece 3 extends at least ¼" beyond both ends of the placement line. Start the machine and allow the tacking line to stitch. Slip a pressing pad under the hoop. Flip the fabric back and fuse it in place with the mini iron.

Refer to the fabric placement chart for the sequence. Repeat this process until all twenty-five pieces have been placed.

10 Start your machine and allow a tacking line square to stitch. Remove the hoop from the machine.

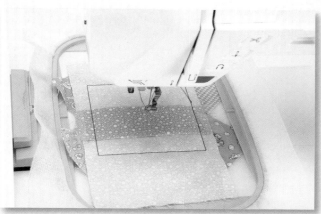

11 Take both 2½" × 4½" pieces of pink backing fabric and fold down the top edge of each by ½", wrong sides together, so that each piece now measures 2" × 4½". Position the two pieces over the project, right sides down, with the folded edges overlapping in the middle of the block. The fabric should extend beyond the tacking line by a minimum of ¼" on all sides. Secure with tape, especially at the overlapping folded edges.

12 Return the hoop to the machine. Start the machine and allow the final tacking line to stitch. This will secure the overlapping fabrics to the finished block.

13 Remove the project from the hoop. Remove the tape. Using a rotary cutter, trim away the excess, leaving ¼" around the edges. Clip the corners.

14 Turn the project inside out, using a point turner to help turn the corners. With the backing side up, neatly press the project.

15 Stuff the pincushion with superfine steel wool or fiberfill.

> Pincushions are traditionally filled with emery sand, which helps keep needles sharp. If you can locate emery sand, make a bag to fit inside the pincushion, fill it with this sand and slipstitch the bag closed. Place the bag inside the pincushion and enjoy sharp needles and pins!

NOTES FROM NANCY

Love Placard

If you look closely, you'll see that this Pineapple design is a little different. I have removed four fabric pieces from the middle to give us more room to embroider in the centers. You can modify the design by changing the letters. This would make a nice house warming gift if you add the new home owner's last name, or you could stitch a placard in Christmas colors with the words *Peace*, *Love* or *Joy*.

13" × 31"

FABRIC & THREAD

FABRIC FOR BLOCKS

Twenty strips in various shades of pink, 1" wide and up to 3" long *[17]*

Four white 4" squares for the centers

Corners 16 2×3 rec

FABRIC FOR SASHING

Five pink 2" × 6" strips

Two pink 2" × 27" strips

FABRIC FOR BORDERS

Two pink 3½" × 33" strips

Two pink 3½" × 15" strips

Two white 1½" × 7½" strips, folded in half

Two white 1½" × 27" strips, folded in half

FABRIC FOR BACKING

One 15" × 33" rectangle

FABRIC FOR BINDING

One 6" × 40" strip

BATTING

One 15" × 33" rectangle

THREAD

Embroidery thread (pink)

Neutral cotton thread for piecing

EMBROIDERY DESIGNS

pinelovee

pinelovel

pineloveo

pinelovev

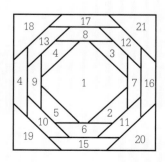

PINEAPPLE PLACARD
FABRIC PLACEMENT CHART

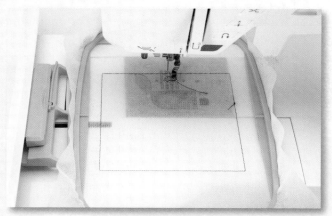

1 Load the designs onto the machine, and pull up the first design (pinelovel). Thread the machine with embroidery thread. Hoop the stabilizer. Start the machine and allow the reference shape to stitch.

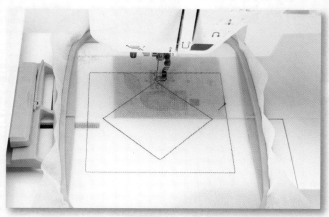

2 Start the machine and allow the placement shape to stitch.

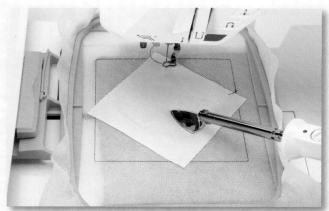

3 Place a 4" white square over the placement shape. Make sure it covers the entire shape. Slip a pressing pad under the hoop, then fuse the fabric in place with the mini iron. Remove the pressing pad.

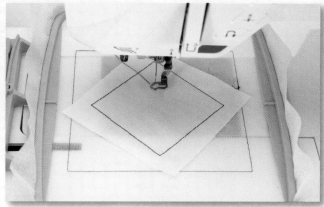

4 Start the machine and allow the tacking line to stitch. This extra step prevents the fabric from puckering when the embroidery design is applied.

5 Remove the hoop from the machine. Using curved scissors, trim as close to the tacking line as possible.

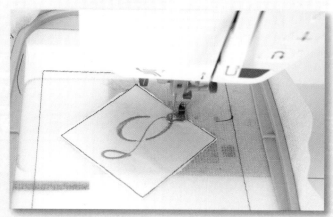

6 Return the hoop to the machine. Start the machine and allow the satin stitching to run.

7 Now begins the stitch-n-flip section of this design. Please refer to the fabric placement chart on page 108 for the stitching order. When the letter has finished stitching, change to neutral thread and allow a placement line to stitch.

8 Place piece 2 right side down along the placement line. Ensure that piece 2 extends at least ¼" beyond both ends of the placement line. Start the machine and allow the tacking line to stitch.

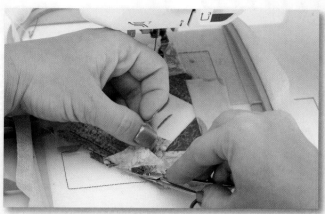

9 Slip a pressing pad under the hoop. Flip the fabric back and use the mini iron to fuse the piece back. Remove the pressing pad.

10 Repeat these steps until all twenty-one pieces have been placed. It is especially important to trim the excess fabric away as you go. The Pineapple block has many pieces, so the seams can get very bulky if you do not trim the fabric.

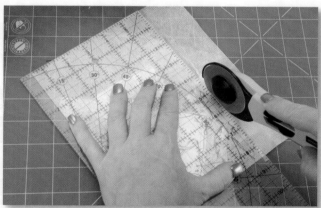

11 When the block has finished stitching, remove it from the hoop. Flip it over. Using a rotary cutter and a quilter's ruler, trim ¼" outside the reference square.

    Create the remaining blocks using the other three designs.

The Pineapple block is a very intricate design. With Larisa's accurate digitized stitching lines, even a novice quilter or embroiderer can create a perfectly pieced Pineapple block the first time!

Putting the Project Together

When you're ready to put the project together, switch to your sewing machine.

Attach 2" sashing all around the letters, trimming the excess. Sew them together in the correct order.

Take the folded white strips and stitch down with folds pointing towards the inside and overlapping the pink sashing. Add a 3½" border. Trim the excess.

Sandwich the backing, batting and top together and stitch down the seams to quilt the three together. Trim the excess and add the binding.

Apron

Once you know how to piece in the hoop, you can add quilt blocks to anything! By adding satin stitching to the finished edge, you can transfer these quilt blocks to just about any surface. Add them to jeans, a jacket or even a scarf. Let's piece some directly on a purchased apron!

FABRIC & THREAD
FABRIC FOR BLOCKS

Crazy Patch

Eight scraps, approximately 1½" × 3½" each

Heart

One 1¾" × 2½" rectangle

Three 1¾" squares for the top corners

Three 1" × 3¾" strips

Two 2" × 3¼" rectangles for the bottom corners

Pineapple

One 2½" square for the center

Twenty-one strips, 1" wide and up to 3" long

Four 1½" × 3" rectangles for the corners

THREAD

Neutral thread for piecing

Embroidery thread for satin stitching

OTHER

Purchased apron

EMBROIDERY DESIGNS

combapr1

combapr2

combapr3

combapr4

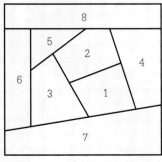

CRAZY PATCH BLOCK FABRIC PLACEMENT CHART

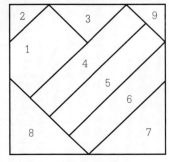

HEART BLOCK FABRIC PLACEMENT CHART

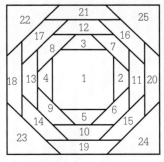

PINEAPPLE BLOCK FABRIC PLACEMENT CHART

1 Load your designs (combapr1 through combapr4) onto the embroidery machine. Thread the machine using either piecing or embroidery thread. Hoop the stabilizer. Locate where you want to place the first block, and then fuse your apron to the stabilizer so that this spot is centered on the hoop. You can also use pins to help secure the apron to the stabilizer.

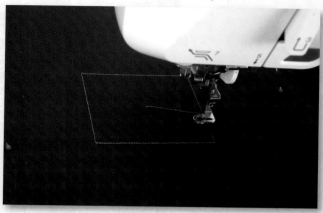

2 Pull up the Crazy Patch design (combapr1). Start the machine and allow the reference shape to stitch out.

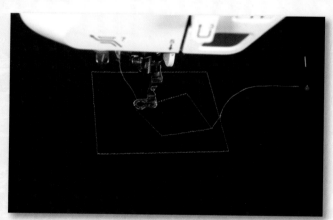

3 Start the machine and allow the placement shape to stitch.

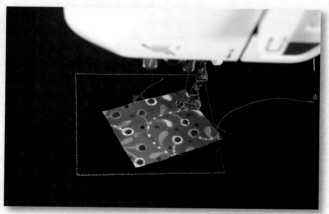

4 Place piece 1 right side up over the placement shape. Start the machine and allow a placement line to stitch.

In this project, you'll be piecing directly on the apron. Instead of using spray adhesive to adhere the first fabric in place, use an ordinary glue stick to temporarily adhere the fabric to the apron. The glue dries clear and crisp; it's a great pinning substitute!

NOTES FROM NANCY

113

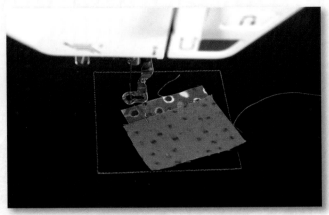

5 Place piece 2 right side down along the placement line. Ensure that piece 2 extends at least ¼" beyond both ends of the placement line. Start the machine and allow a tacking line to stitch.

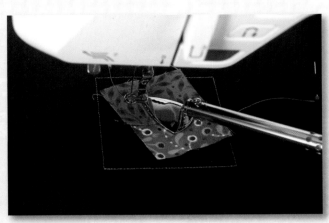

6 Place a pressing pad under the hoop. Using the mini iron, press back piece 2. Remove the pressing pad.

7 Repeat the stitch-n-flip process until all eight pieces are in place.

8 Start the machine and allow a tacking line to stitch around the block.

9 Remove the hoop from the machine. Using your curved scissors, trim as close to the tacking line as possible.

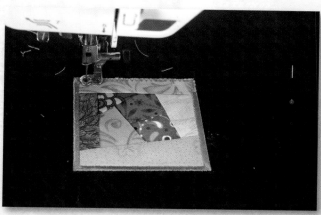

10 Return the hoop to the machine. Start the machine and allow the satin stitching to run.

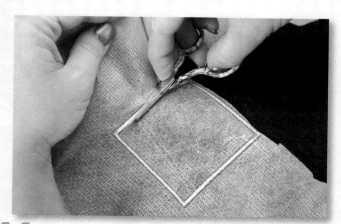

11 Remove the apron from the hoop, turn it over, and trim away the excess stabilizer around the block.

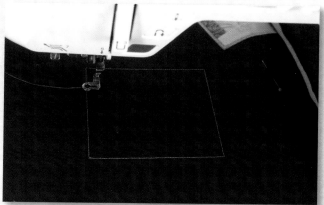

12 When you are ready to place the next block, hoop the stabilizer. Locate where you want to place the block, and then fuse your apron to the stabilizer so that this spot is centered on the hoop. You can also use pins to help secure the apron to the stabilizer. Pull up the Heart design (combapr2). Start the machine and allow the reference shape to stitch out.

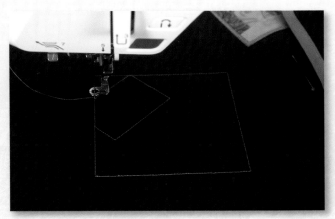

13 Start the machine and allow the placement shape to stitch out.

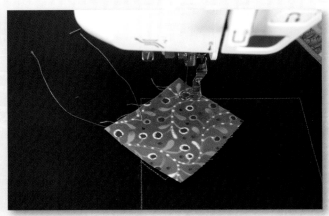

14 Place piece 1 right side up over the placement shape. Start the machine and allow a placement line to stitch.

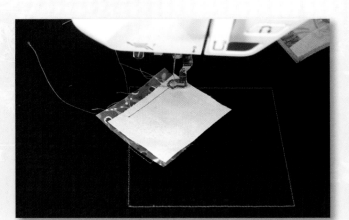

15 Place piece 2 right side down along the placement line. Ensure that piece 2 extends at least ¼" beyond both ends of the placement line. Start the machine and allow a tacking line to stitch.

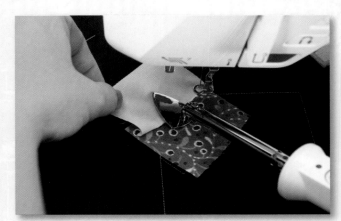

16 Place a pressing pad under the hoop. Using the mini iron, press back piece 2. Remove the pressing pad.

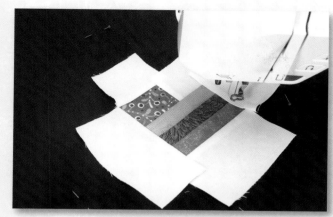

17 Repeat the stitch-n-flip process until all nine pieces are in place.

18 Start the machine and allow a tacking line to stitch around the block. Remove the hoop from the machine. Using your curved scissors, trim as close to the tacking line as possible.

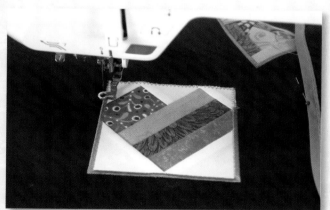

19 Return the hoop to the machine. Start the machine and allow the satin stitching to run.

Remove the apron from the hoop, turn it over and trim away the excess stabilizer around the block.

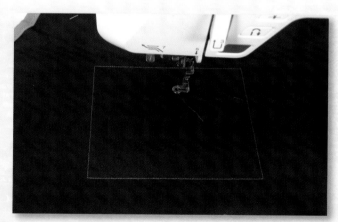

20 When you are ready the place the next block, hoop the stabilizer. Locate where you want to place the block, and then fuse your apron to the stabilizer so that this spot is centered on the hoop. You can also use pins to help secure the apron to the stabilizer. Pull up the Pineapple design (combapr3). Start the machine and allow the reference shape to stitch out.

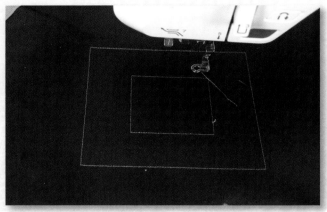

21 Start the machine and allow the placement shape to stitch out.

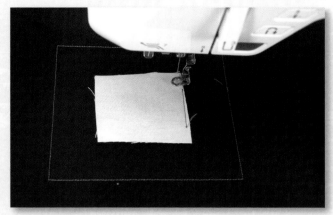

22 Place piece 1 right side up over the placement shape. Start the machine and allow a placement line to stitch.

23 Place piece 2 right side down along the placement line. Ensure that piece 2 extends at least ¼" beyond both ends of the placement line. Start the machine and allow a tacking line to stitch.

24 Place a pressing pad under the hoop. Using the mini iron, press back piece 2. Remove the pressing pad.

25 Repeat the stitch-n-flip process until all twenty-five pieces are in place.

26 Start the machine and allow a tacking line to stitch around the block. Remove the hoop from the machine. Using your curved scissors, trim as close to the tacking line as possible.

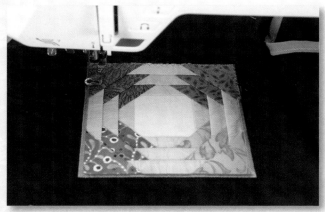

27 Return the hoop to the machine. Start the machine and allow the satin stitching to run.

Remove the apron from the hoop, turn it over and trim away the excess stabilizer around the block.

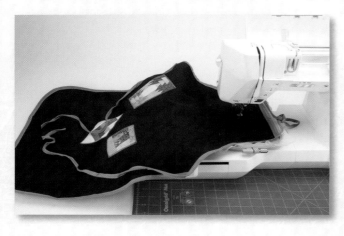

28 If you'd like to add the text, hoop the stabilizer and position the apron to center the text. Fuse the apron to the stabilizer, and pin to help secure it.

29 Pull up the design (combapr4). Start the machine and allow the text to stitch.

30 Using tweezers and your curved scissors, trim away the jump threads.

Candle Covers

I have passed by seven-day candles in the grocery store for years and finally decided to make a craft with them. (These candles are also available online. Search for *7-day candle*.)

Each of these Candle covers are made in only one hooping. You will end up with nice, finished edges, so once you turn it inside out you can just slide it on the candle. The pieced designs are placed at stair-step intervals to make a pleasing arrangement when they're used as a trio. They look really nice sitting on the Candle Placemat (see page 99).

FABRIC & THREAD

FABRIC FOR BLOCKS

Log Cabin

One 1" square for the center

Twelve strips, ½" wide and up to 2¼" long

Two 1½" × 2½" strips for the side borders

Two 4" × 4½" rectangles for the top and bottom borders

Heart

One 1" × 1½" rectangle

Three 1" squares for the top corners

Three ¾" × 2" strips

Two 1½" squares for the bottom corners

Two 1½" × 2½" rectangles for the side borders

One 4½" × 5" rectangles for the top border

One 2½" × 4½" rectangle for the bottom border

Economy

One 1½" square for the center

Four 1" × 1½" rectangles for the inner triangles

Four 1" × 2" rectangles for the outer triangles

Two 1½" × 2½" rectangles for the side borders

One 2½" × 4½" rectangle for the top border

One 4½" × 5" rectangle for the bottom border

FABRIC FOR BACKING

Three 4½" × 9" rectangles to match each holder

THREAD

Neutral thread for piecing

EMBROIDERY DESIGNS

candleecon

candleheart

candlelogcabn

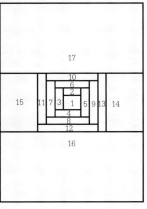

LOG CABIN PATCH FABRIC
PLACEMENT CHART

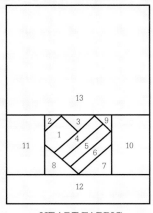

HEART FABRIC
PLACEMENT CHART

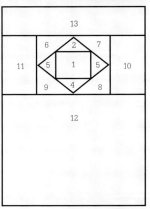

ECONOMY PATCH FABRIC
PLACEMENT CHART

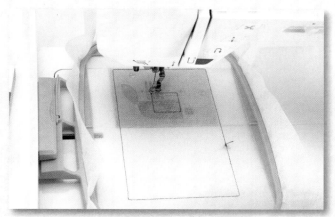

1 Load the designs onto the machine. Hoop the stabilizer. Thread the machine using a neutral thread for piecing. (I've used black here for visibility.) Pull up the Economy Patch (candleecon). Start the machine and allow the reference shape and the placement shape to stitch.

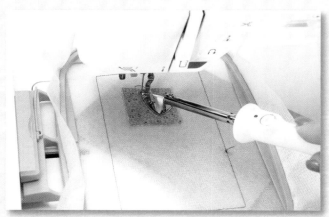

2 Lay piece 1 right side up over the placement shape. Slip a pressing pad under the hoop and use your mini iron to fuse the fabric in place.

3 Start the machine and allow a placement line to stitch.

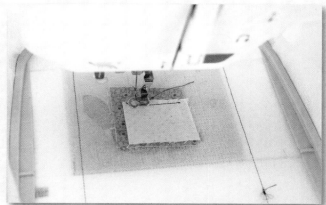

4 Lay piece 2 right side down along the placement line. Ensure that piece 2 extends at least ¼" beyond both ends of the placement line. Start the machine and allow a tacking line to stitch. Trim away the excess fabric.

5 Slip a pressing pad under the hoop. Flip back piece 2 and fuse it in place with the mini iron.

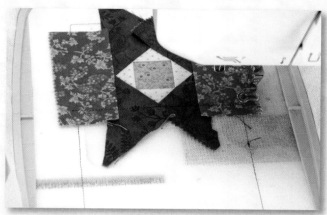

6 Continue with the stitch-n-flip process until eleven pieces are placed. Start the machine and allow a placement line to stitch.

7 Place the 4½" × 2½" rectangle right side down along the placement line. Ensure that the rectangle extends at least ¼" beyond both ends of the placement line. Start the machine and allow the tacking line to stitch. Remove the hoop and trim away the excess fabric.

If you have any loose threads popping up in the block, use tweezers to pull the thread taut and clip it with appliqué scissors as close to the fabric as you can.

NOTES FROM NANCY

123

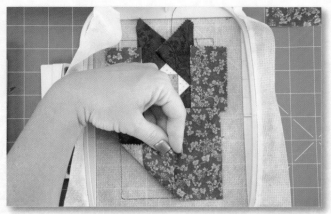

8 Fold the edge under so that it extends just beyond the reference shape line. Press to crease the fabric and fuse it to the stabilizer.

9 Return the hoop to the machine and allow a placement line to stitch.

10 Place the 4½" × 5" rectangle right side down along the placement line. Ensure that the rectangle extends at least ¼" beyond both ends of the placement line. Start the machine and allow the tacking line to stitch. Remove the hoop and trim away the excess fabric.

11 Fold the edge under so that it extends just beyond the reference shape line. Press to fuse it to the stabilizer.

12 Place a 4½" × 9" backing piece of fabric right side down over the project. Fold the edges back, making sure that all the folded edges are aligned to the same height. Press with a mini iron.

Tape the pieces in place. Make sure to apply tape along the folds to hold them securely in place.

13 Return the hoop to the machine and allow the final two lines to stitch. These lines will double back at the ends to give the candle cover added reinforcement at the edges. Remove the project from the hoop and trim away the excess fabric.

14 Trim a "scoop" out of the stabilizer on both ends of the project. This ensures that no stabilizer will show.

15 Turn the project inside out, press, and insert a seven-day candle.

Repeat all these steps for the Heart and Log Cabin designs.

To access the embroidery designs on the DVD, place this DVD into your computer's DVD-rom drive. Open the DVD by double clicking the DVD icon (Mac), or selecting "Open folder to view files" from the pop-up window (PC). The embroidery files are located in the Embroidery Patterns folder.

Crazy Patch
crazypatch

Snowball Project Files

Chicken & Quilt Blocks
snowchik1
snowchik2
snowchik3
snowchik4
snowchikmtf

Fussy-Cut Fabric Blocks
snowfusscut

Valance
snowvalance

Sunshine & Shadows Project Files

Quick-Stitch Scrappy Quilt
sunscrappy

Bookmark
sunbkmrk

Pressing Pad
sunpresspad

Economy Patch Project Files

Quilter's Pouch
econpouch

Welcome Banner
econbannerC
econbannerE
econbannerL
econbannerM
econbannerO
econbannerW

Pillow with Fleur-de-Lys Appliqué
econpillow1
econpillow2

Heart Project Files

Miniature Quilt
heartmini1
heartmini2

Frame Cover
heartframe

Kitchen Towel
hearttowel1
hearttowel2

Log Cabin Project Files

Pillow with Rooster Appliqué
logcabnpill1
logcabnpill2

Itty Bitty Ornament
logcabnorn

Quilt Label
logcabnlabel

Pineapple Project Files

Love Placard
pineloveE
pineloveL
pineloveO
pineloveV

Candle Placemat
pinemat

Pincushion
pinepincush

Combined Techniques

Apron
combapr1
combapr2
combapr3
combapr4

Candle Covers
candleecon
candleheart
candlelogcabn

Bonus Quilting Designs
bonusqdes1
bonusqdes2

Resources

RNK Distributing
Floriani stabilizer, embroidery thread & digitizing software (www.rnkdistributing.com)

OLFA®
Rotary cutters, replacement blades, ¼" quilter's ruler cutting mats (www.olfa.com)

United Notions
Assorted Moda fabrics including Moda Marbles (www.unitednotions.com)

RJR Fabric
1930's prints and other assorted fabrics (www.rjrfabrics.com)

Blank Quilting
Designer Hoodie's chicken fabric on cover of book (www.blankquilting.com)

Havel's Inc.
Curved Scissors, seam rippers (www.havelsewing.com)

June Tailor, Inc.
Cutting mats, ironing board covers, pressing mats (www.junetailor.com)

Superior Threads
Quilting thread; SoFINE! #50 cream (www.superiorthreads.com)

Clover Needlecraft Inc.
9101 Mini Iron II (www.clover-usa.com/)

Buzz Tools
BuzzXplore for embroidery conversions (www.buzztools.com)

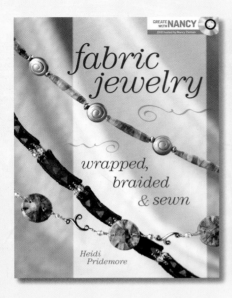

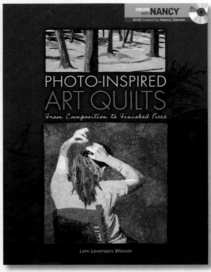

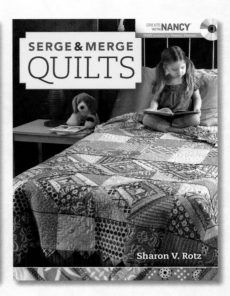

Fabric Jewelry Wrapped, Braided & Sewn

Heidi Pridemore and Nancy Zieman

Make stunning beads and accessories using fabrics and fibers. Heidi includes instructions for making 17 types of beads and 5 types of chains, plus she shows you how to incorporate them into 20 projects.

paperback, 128 pages
ISBN-10: 1-4402-0250-8
ISBN-13: 978-1-4402-0250-6
Z4823

Photo-Inspired Art Quilts From Composition to Finished Piece

Leni Levenson Wiener and Nancy Zieman

Starting with nothing but fabric and a photo, learn to create a fabulous art quilt! Leni gives you all the tools you need for the entire process, from composition to bound-and-finished piece.

paperback, 128 pages
ISBN-10: 0-89689-804-0
ISBN-13: 978-0-89689-804-2
Z2873

Serge & Merge Quilts

Sharon V. Rotz and Nancy Zieman

Serging meets quilting in this title from the Create with Nancy series. Use your serger to both create and embellish 15 different quilt projects. Break out your serger and get quilting!

paperback, 128 pages
ISBN-10: 0-89689-810-5
ISBN-13: 978-0-89689-810-3
Z2917

All of these wonderful titles include a bonus DVD, hosted by Nancy Zieman, that let you see the techniques in action! In addition, Nancy's Notes are sprinkled throughout the books, giving you extra tips and advice on how to create the best project you can!

These and other fine Krause Publications titles are available at your local craft retailer, bookstore or online supplier, or visit our Web site at www.mycraftivitystore.com.